NECESSARY CHANGES:

Dr John R. Adolph

This book is dedicated to

Jesus Christ and His finished work on the Cross

To devout believers in the Lord, whose human doubt, dismay, and disbelief demands and necessitates the Cross of Christ and the grace of God

To sincere followers of Jesus Christ, who have made up their minds to follow Him and leave the world behind them

To active Sunday morning worshippers who desire a deeper, more meaningful understanding of God's Word

To in-active church members around the world who peeped into the window of a local assembly of Christians and found liberalism, legalism, religious hypocrisy, and not God's redemptive love

To pastors who have been called by the Lord of the Cross to preach the Gospel but have somehow missed preaching, teaching, and sharing the truth regarding the subject of repentance

To every real Christian who can say, "I love the Lord with everything in me, and yet, I still struggle from time to time while under the sanctified reconstruction of the Lord."

NECESSARY CHANGES:
THE NEED AND POWER OF REPENTANCE

Dr. John R. Adolph

Necessary Changes: The Need and Power of Repentance by Dr. John R. Adolph
Copyright © 2025 by John R. Adolph
All Rights Reserved.
ISBN: 978-1-59755-833-4

Published by: ADVANTAGE BOOKS™, Orlando, FL
www.advbookstore.com

All Rights Reserved. This book and parts thereof may not be reproduced in any form, stored in a retrieval system or transmitted in any form by any means (electronic, mechanical, photocopy, recording or otherwise) without prior written permission of the author, except as provided by United States of America copyright law.
Scriptures quotations taken from the Holy Bible KING JAMES VERSION (KJV), public domain.

Library of Congress Catalog Number: 2025937199

Name:	Adolph, John R., Author
Title:	*Necessary Changes: The Need and Power of Repentance*
	John R. Adolph
	Advantage Books, 2024
Identifiers:	ISBN Paperback: 9781597558334
	ISBN eBook: 9781597558396
Subjects:	Books › Religion & Spirituality › Worship & Devotion Devotionals
	Books › Religion & Spirituality › Worship & Devotion Inspirational
	Books › Religion & Spirituality › Worship & Devotion Prayer

First Printing: May 2025
25 26 27 28 29 30 31   10 9 8 7 6 5 4 3 2 1

Table of Contents

ACKNOWLEDGEMENTS 11
PREFACE 13
FOREWORD 15
INTRODUCTION 17
ONE WORD THAT CHANGES EVERYTHING THE MEANING OF REPENTANCE 19

Week 1: Make A U-Turn And Keep Straight (2 Chronicles 7:14)

DAY 1: IF AND ONLY IF 27
DAY 2: THIS IS A VERY PERSONAL MATTER 28
DAY 3: THERE'S ONE PRAYER GOD ALWAYS ACCEPTS 29
DAY 4: OCEAN, ABOUT-FACE 30
DAY 5: TRUST ME, HEAVEN HAS THE ANSWER 31
DAY 6: GOOD NEWS, THE JUDGE SAYS YOU'RE FREE TO GO 32
DAY 7: FORGIVEN, HEALED AND BLESSED 33
WEEK 1 CONCLUSION 34

Week 2: The Day God Changed His Mind (Jonah 3:10)

DAY 1: WHAT YOU DO REALLY MATTERS 35
DAY 2: WHEN THE PUNISHMENT DOES NOT FIT THE CRIME 36
DAY 3: YOUR EVIL DAYS AND YOUR EVIL WAYS 37
DAY 4: HE DID NOT HAVE TO DO IT, BUT HE DID 38
DAY 5: SOME THINGS DO CHANGE 39
DAY 6: WHEN YOU CHANGED YOURS, HE CHANGED HIS 40
DAY 7: HE DID NOT DO IT 41
WEEK 2 CONCLUSION 42

Week 3: Change Your Mind About Me (St. Matthew 22:41-42

DAY 1: I'VE GOT A QUESTION FOR YOU 43
DAY 2: THE BLESSING OF A CHEAT SHEET 44
DAY 3: SO CLOSE, BUT YET SO FAR 45
DAY 4: HE'S JUST THE SON OF GOD RIGHT? 46
DAY 5: YOU'VE GOT THE RIGHT ONE 47

DAY 6: THERE'S NOBODY QUITE LIKE HIM 48
DAY 7: EVERYTHING CHANGES WHEN YOU CHANGE YOUR MIND ABOUT HIM 49
WEEK 3 CONCLUSION 50

Week 4: Citizenship Really Matters (St. Matthew 4:17)

DAY 1: THE FIRST WORDS ALWAYS MEAN THE MOST 51
DAY 2: THERE'S A NEW KING IN TOWN 52
DAY 3: IT'S OUT WITH THE OLD AND IN WITH THE NEW 53
DAY 4: IMMIGRATION REFORM 54
DAY 5: LAWS OF THE KINGDOM OF GOD 55
DAY 6: NOT GREEN CARDS, BUT BIRTH CERTIFICATES 56
DAY 7: CITIZENSHIP HAS ITS PRIVILEGES 57
WEEK 4 CONCLUSION 58

Week 5: It's Do Or Die (St. Luke 13:1-3)

DAY 1: IF YOU DON'T DO IT, YOU'LL DIE 59
DAY 2: IF YOU DO IT, YOU'LL LIVE 60
DAY 3: TO SAY IT AND NOT DO IT IS DANGEROUS 61
DAY 4: DECISIONS, DECISIONS, DECISIONS 62
DAY 5: SOME THINGS GOT TO CHANGE 63
DAY 6: WHAT DOES IT MEAN TO PERISH? 64
DAY 7: MY MIND'S MADE UP, NO TURNING BACK 65
WEEK 5 CONCLUSION 66

Week 6: Thank God, He Gave Me A Chance To Change (St. Luke 19:8-10)

DAY 1: WE KEEP COMING UP SHORT 67
DAY 2: EVEN IF YOU CLIMB A TREE, YOU STILL CAN'T FIX YOUR PROBLEM 68
DAY 3: HE KNOWS YOUR SINS BUT CALLS YOU BY YOUR NAME 69
DAY 4: GOD'S LOVE CHANGES EVERYTHING 70
DAY 5: I'M SORRY, I WAS WRONG AND I KNOW IT 71
DAY 6: ACTIONS SPEAK LOUDER THAN WORDS 72
DAY 7: WHEN SHORT PEOPLE MAKE TALL CHANGES 73
WEEK 6 CONCLUSION 74

Week 7: It's Hot In Here (St. Luke 16:30)

DAY 1: THERE ARE SOME THINGS MONEY CAN'T BUY 75
DAY 2: CONTRARY TO POPULAR OPINION, HELL IS REAL 76
DAY 3: ONCE IT'S OVER YOU CAN'T GO BACK 77
DAY 4: SOME PEOPLE WILL NEVER CHANGE 78
DAY 5: FIVE THINGS ABOUT HELL YOU SHOULD NEVER FORGET 79
DAY 6: DEATH IS NOT A THREAT, IT'S A REALITY 80
DAY 7: IT'S JUST FOR THOSE WHO REFUSE TO CHANGE 81
WEEK 7 CONCLUSION 82

Week 8: He Changed My Life Forever (St. Mark 5:15)

DAY 1: DEMONS CAN DO DAMAGE 83
DAY 2: HE'S VICIOUS TO SOME BUT HE'S A VESSEL TO THE LORD ... 84
DAY 3: A PICTURE IS WORTH A THOUSAND WORDS 85
DAY 4: A DECISION THAT CHANGES YOUR CONDITION 86
DAY 5: YOU DO YOUR PART AND HE'LL DO HIS 87
DAY 6: CLOTHED IN YOUR RIGHT MIND 88
DAY 7: WHAT A WONDERFUL CHANGE 89
WEEK 8 CONCLUSION 90

Week 9: Three Strikes And You're In (St. Mark 16:5-7)

DAY 1: HE MISSED IT THREE TIMES 91
DAY 2: THANK GOD HE DIDN'T GIVE UP ON YOU 92
DAY 3: TO KNOW BETTER IS ONE THING TO DO BETTER IS ANOTHER 93
DAY 4: O TO BE KEPT BY JESUS 94
DAY 5: GOD SAYS, CHANGE YOUR MIND ABOUT ME 95
DAY 6: REPENTANCE AND FORGIVENESS GO TOGETHER 96
DAY 7: GOOD NEWS YOU'RE STILL ON THE TEAM 97
WEEK 9 CONCLUSION 98

Week 10: I'll Never Be The Same Again (Acts 9:3-4)

DAY 1: SOME CHANGE REQUIRES CONFRONTATION 99
DAY 2: LORD, WHAT DO YOU WANT ME TO DO 100
DAY 3: EYES WITH NO VISION 101
DAY 4: RESTORATION: GOD ALWAYS HAS A PLAN 102

DAY 5: A STREET CALLED STRAIGHT 103
DAY 6: GOOD NEWS, U-TURNS ALLOWED... 104
DAY 7: RELIGION IS ONE THING, BUT REPENTANCE IS SOMETHING ELSE.......... 105
WEEK 10 CONCLUSION 106

Week 11: The Answer Is Knocking (Rev. 3:19-20)

DAY 1: DON'T YOU HEAR HIM KNOCKING 107
DAY 2: IT'S RUDE NOT TO ANSWER THE DOOR 108
DAY 3: HE'S KNOCKING BECAUSE HE WANTS TO GET BACK IN 109
DAY 4: WHO GAVE GOD AN EVICTION NOTICE... 110
DAY 5: HURRY UP AND HANDLE YOUR BUSINESS 111
DAY 6: GET OFF THE FENCE... 112
DAY 7: TRUST ME; HE'S NOT SOLICITING 113
WEEK 11 CONCLUSION 114

Week 12: But What Do You Say? (St. Matthew 16:13)

DAY 1: EVERYBODY HAS AN OPINION, I WANT TO KNOW YOURS........................ 115
DAY 2: HE SAY, SHE SAY, THEY SAY, HEARSAY 116
DAY 3: THIS POP QUIZ ONLY HAS ONE QUESTION ON IT 117
DAY 4: IF YOU DON'T KNOW, NOW YOU KNOW 118
DAY 5: CHANGE HAPPENS WHEN YOUR MIND SHIFTS 119
DAY 6: THE HOLY GHOST GETS THE GLORY FOR THIS ONE................................ 120
DAY 7: THE REAL CHANGE AGENT IS GOD 121
WEEK 12 CONCLUSION 122

Week 13: Trying To Fix It By Yourself Can Kill You (St. Matthew 27:3)

DAY 1: JUDAS WASN'T A BAD GUY 123
DAY 2: THE ONE PROBLEM YOU WILL NEVER BE ABLE TO FIX 124
DAY 3: REFUSE TO BE A SELL-OUT 125
DAY 4: HOW MUCH DOES YOUR CHRIST COST 126
DAY 5: TURN TO GOD 127
DAY 6: DON'T LET THE MISTAKES OF YOUR PAST ERASE FUTURE BLESSINGS. 128
DAY 7: REPENTANCE SAYS HE CAN FIX IT 129
WEEK 13 CONCLUSION 130

Week 14: They Wouldn't, So He Didn't (St. Matthew 11:20)

DAY 1: SOMEBODY IS IN TROUBLE, AND I DON'T WANT IT TO BE ME 131
DAY 2: THERE'S A REASON WHY RELIGIOUS PEOPLE DON'T REPENT 132
DAY 3: PRACTICE DOES NOT ALWAYS MAKE PERFECT 133
DAY 4: IT'S NOT A COMMAND, IT'S A SUGGESTION 135
DAY 5: "TO BE OR NOT TO BE" IS NOT THE REAL QUESTION 136
DAY 6: IF YOU DON'T, GOD WON'T 137
DAY 7: IT'S HARD BUT FAIR, SAD BUT TRUE 138
WEEK 14 CONCLUSION 139

Week 15: All You Have To Do Is RSVP (2 Peter 3:9)

DAY 1: THE INVITATIONS HAVE GONE OUT 140
DAY 2: HE'S A PROMISE KEEPER 141
DAY 3: I'M STILL WAITING 142
DAY 4: YOUR CHANCE TO CHANGE COULD BE HAPPENING RIGHT NOW 143
DAY 5: WHEN YOU TRANSLATE THE WORD "ALL" IT MEANS "ALL" 145
DAY 6: SOME PEOPLE JUST WON'T ACT RIGHT 146
DAY 7: DELIVERANCE WORKS BEST WHEN YOU COOPERATE 148
WEEK 15 CONCLUSION 149

Dr John R. Adolph

ACKNOWLEDGEMENTS

When I was a younger Pastor, I often said "yes" to almost every communal engagement that I was invited to and every pulpit assignment that came my way. In short, I put the "B" in busy. At one point in my ministry, I was preaching forty eight crusades, symposiums or plenaries a year. It was beyond sensible. One hot Texas summer day, I picked up a book that changed my philosophy of how I use my God-given gift of time on Earth. I was blessed to read <u>Essentialism: The Disciplined Pursuit of Less</u> by Greg McKeown, and the madness stopped. I was blessed to discover that saying "no" is not a sin. Saying "no" is a complete sentence.

Along with my newfound discovery of saying "no" came a more profound, more meaningful desire for me to say "yes" to the will of God. With this desire in my heart, I realized just how important the Great Commission (St. Matthew 28:16-20), the Great Commandment (St. Matthew 22:35-40), and the Great Calling (St. Matthew 4:19) of Jesus Christ are to the church. When I realized how vital these commandments were to the church of God on earth, I made them the core values of the Antioch Church of Beaumont, Texas. We recite them every Sunday, and we live by them every day as a church family. In this stead, I also realized how important it is for me to teach, preach, share, and declare primary doctrinal truths of the Christian faith with believers and non-believers around the world.

With this in mind, I began studying, gaining, preaching, teaching, learning, writing and publishing like never before. As I said "no" to things that were not truly important to me, I found the time to say "yes" to sharing the life-changing truths given to us as believers in God's Word. Writing takes time and works, like the one you now hold in your hand, took a team of people to help it come to fruition. In this stead, I must acknowledge and appreciate my amazing wife and mother of my children, Lady Dorrie Adolph, whose steadfast love, care, commitment, and consolation push me forward in the faith of our Lord Jesus Christ. To my kids, Sumone and Jonathan, who decided to give their lives to Jesus Christ as children and today as young adults, continue to serve Him as their Lord and Savior. I appreciate my Executive Director, Minister Brooklyn Williams, who faithfully supports each of my literary endeavors as if they were her own. I am sincerely thankful to my Executive Church Leaders, Sister Felicia Young, Dr. Karen Davis, and Rev. Jamison Malbrough, for their personal push for me to write and publish this book.

Dr John R. Adolph

I am humbled by Executive Church Officers: Deacons, Trustees, Clergy, Coordinators, Directors, and Lay Leaders who share with me weekly and encourage my soul daily to keep teaching God's Word. I am blessed with the most incredible day staff in the world who help me share God's love with people from their desks daily: Pastor Albert Moore, Minister Kim Hardy, Sister Deandra Darby, and Minister Linda Jones. I am so grateful for my tenured Staff Leaders: Jewel "Sue" Cooper, Lorraine Lemons, Pastor Jack Gay, Rev. Major M. Goldman III, and Rev. Alfred Beverly II who have remained with me over the years who have helped me build the current Antioch.

Most importantly, I must thank God for the time, toil, and talent of a group of young people who emerged as the heroes of the pandemic for the church and helped us to keep sharing the Gospel Message around the world virtually. Hats off to my Media Ministry and Media Team. Special thanks to Dr. Porchanee' White and Sister Lori Ceasar for editing and transcribing this work so that literary excellence would be the end result for every reader that would pursue its pages.

PREFACE

It is undeniably true that Dr. John Adolph is a prolific preacher, dynamic pastor, spiritual leader, and business extraordinaire of our time. In his book Necessary Changes, he challenges the body of Christ and the world to repent: A change of mind that leads to a change of behavior and ultimately takes one in a new direction. John the Baptist preached repentance, and ALL of Judea and Jerusalem came to hear him (see Mk.1:4-5), proving that he had a thriving ministry without a watered-down message.

There is now another JOHN," Dr. John Adolph." preaching this same message of repentance. He, too, has a thriving ministry, post-COVID, without a watered-down message. This read is not just a challenge to the body of Christ and the world; it's also a challenge to preachers and pastors to preach God's timeless and eternal truth. We don't have to water down God's message for our ministry to grow.

Thank you, Dr. John Adolph, for this reminder.

Dr. Thomas Beavers
New Rising Star Baptist Church
Birmingham, AL.

Dr John R. Adolph

NECESSARY CHANGES: The Need and Power of Repentance

FOREWORD

There are street signs on every highway, interstate, and rural thoroughfare to give directional clues to aid us in our daily travels. Signs are necessary to ensure our safe arrival to our desired destinations. Stop signs. Dangerous intersection signs. Yield and merge signs – each to prohibit wrecks, which, sadly, often end in fatalities. But the sign that is often the most beneficial on our journey is the U-turn. If we make a wrong turn, it is posted to help us in making a mid-course correction to get back on the right road.

In this seminal work, my friend Dr. John Adolph has given us in bold relief, what a U-turn means to the Christian believer. Genuine repentance begins with a clear understanding of the godly sorrow that produces an earnestness, an eagerness, and a profound sense of ready and willing confession backed by a desire to change one's course of action. Recognition of sin is central to biblical repentance, signaled by a new desire for and experience of the Presence of God.

It is not only a joyful delight to hear John Adolph preach; it is also an enlivening experience to read his thoughts in print. He is mighty in the Scriptures and persuasive in his presentation of the unsearchable riches of God's Word.

Harry Emerson Fosdick tells of a ride-share with a man he did not know in a New York cab. When asked by the driver for his destination, the man wryly retorted, *"How much is the fare to take me back 10 years? I made a wrong turn years ago and I would give anything to go back!"*

Calvary is God's U-turn! If you made a wrong turn, read this book and turn around. REPENT!

Pastor Terry K. Anderson
Lily Grove Missionary Baptist Church
Houston, TX.

Dr John R. Adolph

NECESSARY CHANGES: The Need and Power of Repentance

INTRODUCTION

Nothing comes in touch with God and remains the same. If God is present in the nocturnal darkness of pitch-black midnight, He will speak the words, "Let there be light," and radical change will come to pass because night will be changed to day. If God decides to lift a handful of dirt from the crusted surface of the Earth, when He is finished with it, you will behold the beauty and bounty of the creation of humankind. When God makes contact with a huge bucket of water, it becomes the sweetest wine you have ever tasted. And if a blind man, born with no eyes, meets our Lord, he departs from Him after washing in a pool with a new testimony: I was blind, but now I see!

Change! It's what happens when you meet God, and it's what happens when you use your God-given volitional right to make decisions. Change happens either for the good or for the bad. With this in mind, the subject of repentance means to change. It is here that you find the core, crux, and center of this work. As this work is introduced, it should be noted that the very first word of the Gospel of Jesus Christ, used in the canon, is the term repent, and it means "change."

You live in a culture where people either reject God, because they do not want to change, or they accept the Lord and live as if change is not necessary. However, to be clear, if you are going to be a believer in Jesus Christ, some things are just necessary. Think about it for a moment and consider the fact that some things are necessary for every believer in Christ. For example, it is necessary that you believe in Jesus Christ as Lord and Savior (Acts 16:31), and you get baptized as a sign of your obedience and belief in Him (St. Matthew 28:16-20). Because you believe and are baptized, you are sealed with the Holy Spirit (Eph. 1:13). Not only are you sealed with the Spirit, but you are filled with the Holy Spirit (Ephesians 5:18), and led by the Spirit (Romans 8:14). You seek to be faithful (2 Corinthians 5:7), fruitful (St. John 15:1-7), and forward moving in the faith (Phil. 3:14), you pray (1 Thess. 5:17), persevere in the face of afflictions (Psalms 34:19), and pray and fast from time to time (St. Matthew 17:21). You serve God by serving others. Not so that you can be saved, but because you are saved (St. John 9:1-9). You seek God (St. Matthew 6:33) and give freely because God has graced you with so much (St. Luke 6:38).

Yet, the most fundamental of all of your beliefs is the need and necessity for repentance. This one need is so primal and fundamental that it was the first word that Jesus spoke when He introduced the Kingdom of God on Earth. Repentance, then, is the root of the necessary changes that you should make, face, and embrace as a believer in Jesus Christ. But what is it? How does it work? When does it take place? These questions and many more will be addressed in the pages yet to come.

This book is not a theological treatise on the subject of repentance, though it will closely examine what it is, why it is needed, and how it works. This work is not a lexicon of words that define entirely what repentance is, but it will have a solid look at the term in Hebrew, Aramaic, Greek, Latin and English. This book will not answer every question you may have about the presented subject. However, it will give some solid resolutions that should bless you in many manifold ways that should foster growth and development in the Christian faith. This work will present itself as a daily devotional with one passage that will be studied for an entire week. It will include prayers, parallel scripture readings, and practical moments of application that will be labeled "Higher Than The Top", in which the daily lesson becomes a faith function for you to practice in your Christian walk.

Change is not bad; it is completely necessary!

NECESSARY CHANGES: The Need and Power of Repentance

ONE WORD THAT CHANGES EVERYTHING

THE MEANING OF REPENTANCE

An Etymological Study

To be clear, understanding what repentance means depends largely upon how the term is defined and the context in which it is used. The first step in receiving the Gospel of Jesus Christ is to repent. This study will cover several languages for the purpose of clarity and proper interpretation. First, you will analyze the term in Hebrew, Aramaic, Greek, Latin, and English. Secondly, you will look intently at the use of the word in the Hebrew Scriptures and then look at how the Koine Greek New Testament presents it. Finally, you will look intently at the term repentance in light of the word penitent, to examine its connectedness to this subject matter.

****

Repentance In Hebrew & Aramaic

The Bible consists of sixty-six books, thirty-nine of which are located in the Old Testament. These books of the Bible make up what is called the TANAK, the Torah, Nevi-im, and Kethuvim. In this section of the study, a concentrated focus will be placed on repentance in the Old Testament.

Four words recorded in the Old Testament are used as the term repentance or its derivative. Two terms are central, with one word being dominant. Let's examine all of them.

****

NAHEM
(To feel regret)

This term appears thirty-seven times in the Old Testament. Each time it is mentioned, it comes from the term nahem. It means to feel sorry about a decision or to possess a sincere feeling of regret. It can also mean to feel sad to the point of needing consolation.

According to the Law of First Mention, the first citation of repentance, mentioned in the Bible, is found in Genesis 6:6. It says, "And it repented the LORD that he had made man on the earth, and it grieved him at his heart."

The same word is used in Job 42:6, where the scriptures say," Wherefore I abhor myself, and repent in dust and ashes."

The final mention of repentance, given in the Old Testament, is found in Zech. 9:14, and here is how it reads: "And the LORD shall be seen over them, and his arrow shall go forth as the lightning: and the LORD God shall blow the trumpet and shall go with whirlwinds of the south."

In all of the above references cited, the word for repentance used is nahem.

****

SHOOV
(To return or to turn around)

This word is the most interesting term ever. It is found in the Old Testament three times, and each time it is mentioned, it suggests turning around and moving in the opposite direction. In a military sense, it would be a charge given to a company of soldiers to do an about-face. In context, repentance does not mean just to feel sorry about sin, but to move completely away from it and go in the opposite direction. In a very practical sense, **shoov** means to return to a place or a residence and take a seat. Returning to what you were supposed to be. Into a state you were designed to live within. To return to a place of residence. In short, this is a psychosomatic term that deals with your mind and body.

Here's how the Bible uses this term:

1 Kings 8:47. Yet if they shall bethink themselves in the land whither they were carried captives, and repent, and make supplication unto thee in the land of them that carried them captives, saying, We have sinned, and have done perversely, we have committed wickedness;

Eze. 14:6. Therefore say unto the house of Israel, Thus saith the Lord GOD; Repent, and turn yourselves from your idols; and turn away your faces from all your abominations.

Eze. 18:30. Therefore I will judge you, O house of Israel, every one according to his ways, saith the Lord GOD. Repent, and turn yourselves from all your transgressions; so iniquity shall not be your ruin.

NECESSARY CHANGES: The Need and Power of Repentance

****

HAPHAK
(To change or to turn)

Even though this word is only mentioned once in the Old Testament, its meaning is very significant. It means to change, to turn, to overthrow; however, in this text, based on the Hebrew stem used, it means to comfort. It means to bring comfort like a Father would bring to his own child during times of confusion.

Hosea 11:8. How shall I give thee up, Ephraim? How shall I deliver thee, Israel? How shall I make thee as Admah? How shall I set thee as Zeboim? mine heart is turned within me, my repentings are kindled together.

In this passage, God's compassion and care are put on display towards His people.

****

NOKHAM
(To feel sorry)

Lastly, the Hebrew Scriptures presents to you a term used for repentance that means to feel a sense of sorrow. In this context, this is something that the Lord hides from His people.

Hosea 13:14. I will ransom them from the power of the grave; I will redeem them from death: O death, I will be thy plagues; O grave, I will be thy destruction: repentance shall be hid from mine eyes.

With these brief word studies in mind, a fundamental idea of repentance in the Old Testament is presented.

****

Repentance In The New Testament Scriptures
The New Testament consists of twenty-seven books. These writings include the Gospels, which record for you the life and times of Jesus Christ while He walked the Earth; a history book that chronicles the exciting and dynamic origins of the church; and epistles or letters, written mainly by the Apostle Paul.

The original language of the New Testament is Koine (Common) Greek. With this in mind, four words will be examined in this section. Two of them make up the vast majority of the New Testament meaning of the word "repent". The last two terms are sparsely used.

For the sake of proper interpretation and word meaning, all of the words used for the word repent will be examined in this segment.

****

METANOEO
(To change the mind or direction)

This term is mentioned thirty-two times between Matthew and Revelation, and each time that it is cited, it translates like this: after the change. More specifically, meta means after, and noeo translates into English as change. According to Dr. Wayne Merrit, a posthumous New Testament scholar, this term carries with it substantial socio-political overtones. Metanoeo was used to describe the change of mind and heart that took place when a citizen of one kingdom departed from that king to live under the government of another king and dwell in his kingdom. Of course, there are many other factors to consider when using this paradigm. However, the emphasis is on the change of mind and heart that this word connotes and suggests.

The first mention of this word and its citations in summation are as follows:

St. Matthew 3:1-2. In those days came John the Baptist, preaching in the wilderness of Judaea, and saying, Repent ye: for the kingdom of heaven is at hand.

St. Luke 13:3. I tell you, Nay: but, except ye repent, ye shall all likewise perish.

Revelation 3:19. As many as I love, I rebuke and chasten: be zealous, therefore, and repent.

****

METANOIA
(To change the mind. To change from something to something else)

Metanoia translates into the word repentance twenty-four times, and it presents one of the most powerful terms ever used. This word deals with changing your mind. However, this is not just some casual change. It is not as if you are in a drive-through window ordering fast food and change your mind from option two and order a number four with super large fries. This term is more dominant. It deals emphatically with a change of mind so radical that what is "no longer" and what is "now" is entirely different. A great portrait of this type of radical transformation is seen when the man in the tomb (St. Mark 5:1-11) has an encounter with Jesus Christ, and he is transformed into a man who is no longer wild and untamed but sane and seated in his right mind.

NECESSARY CHANGES: The Need and Power of Repentance

Most importantly, this term suggests that in order for there to be authentic change, it must involve a change from something to something else. By this, it means a change of mind from any and everything else that would keep you from going back to God.

Here are some helpful citations of this word and its usage.

St. Matthew 3:11. I indeed baptize you with water unto repentance, but he that cometh after me is mightier than I, whose shoes I am not worthy to bear: he shall baptize you with the Holy Ghost, and with fire:

St. Luke 5:32. I came not to call the righteous, but sinners to repentance.

2 Corinthians 7:9
Now I rejoice, not that ye were made sorry, but that ye sorrowed to repentance: for ye were made sorry after a godly manner, that ye might receive damage by us in nothing.

****

METAMELOMAI
(To feel sadness or remorse)

This is the third most used term for repentance in the New Testament. It is found six times in the New Testament scriptures, and it means after sorrow or after you feel a sense of remorse. Of course, as in the previous definition, meta translates after, and melomia is where we borrow the English term melancholy. Thus, metamalomia means after you feel a sense of sorrow. With this in mind, true repentance deals emphatically with a godly sorrow for sin.

Listed here are just a few verses that embrace this idea of repentance.

St. Matthew 21:29. He answered and said, I will not: but afterward he repented, and went.

2 Corinthians 7:8. For though I made you sorry with a letter, I do not repent, though I did repent: for I perceive that the same epistle hath made you sorry, though it were but for a season.

Hebrews 7:21. For those priests were made without an oath; but this with an oath by him that said unto him, The Lord sware and will not repent, Thou art a priest for ever After the order of Melchisedec:)

****

AMETAMELITOS
(To be without a changing of the mind)

Even though this word is only mentioned twice in the New Testament, it is very powerful and poignant. It deals with the mind that has not been changed. Notice the alphabet "A" that is cited in its spelling before meta. This presents the idea of being without something. Therefore, this term means to be without a change of mind.

When there is no change of mind, there is no repentance at all.

Romans 11:29. For the gifts and calling of God are without repentance.

2 Corinthians 7:10. For godly sorrow worketh repentance to salvation not to be repented of: but the sorrow of the world worketh death.

****

Repentance In Latin

POENITENTIAM | RESIPISCENTIA | TRANSMENTATIO
(To make a change | To come to your senses | To change your mind)

There is a Latin version of the scriptures called the Vulgate translated by Jerome. In his translation of God's word, he looked at the term repentance and presented three very interesting terms that sought to give it definition.

Based on Jerome's etymology, the following terms are translated into the word repentance.

First of all, there is the word **poenitentim** and it simply means to repent or to change your mind. Nothing more or less is added to this term. The second word adds more color and dimension to the word repent and comes from the Latin term **resipiscentia** and it means to come to your senses. A great example of this usage would be found in the Gospel of Luke, where the Bible speaks of the prodigal son and says, "And when he came to himself…." (St. Luke 15:17a, KJV). This verse finds the prodigal son buried in a pig pen, when all of a sudden, this young man makes a decision to rise from his place of eating with hogs and heads homeward to his father's house. According to this Latin term, he finally came to his senses and decided to go home. In short, he repented.

NECESSARY CHANGES: The Need and Power of Repentance

Lastly, there is the Latin word **transmentatio**. And, like some of the Hebrew and Greek etymological affiliates, it means to have a change of mind.

****

Repentance In English

This word study reveals that the idea of repentance connotes and suggests a sorrowful feeling regarding one's personal past as it pertains to both known and unknown sins. Equally important is a radical change of mind that deals with how you see God, sin, and self as it relates to becoming what the Lord created you to be.

In this stead, the prefix **RE** means to do something again. Even better stated, it means back to or to return to. The root word **PENTA** translates to five. This is why the Pentagon is a five-sided building. And the Pentateuch is the first five books of the Bible. According to the Hebrew word pictures, five is the number of grace in the Biblical text. By the fifth day of creation, humanity had been given everything it would take to sustain life without having to work for it. Thus, to repent is to return to grace.

The root word **PENT** can also refer to a place and a state. In a practical sense, it can refer to an elevated state of existence. In a lecture on repentance, Dr. Myles Monroe argued that the most elevated suite in a hotel is called a PENThouse for this very reason. It's the highest point in the hotel. In this stead, God is calling humanity to the state of existence we had with Him before Adam and Eve did what He commanded them not to do in the Garden.

With this in mind, the resolve regarding repentance is to say that God wants you to reach a point where you are sorrowful about the sins you have committed, to do a complete about-face because your sins are beneath you, and to return to the grace that you find only in Him. This grace, when it is finished with you, elevates you to the original state of being you shared with the Lord before the fall occurred.

The goal, then, of repentance is to cause sinful, flawed, depraved humankind the blessed privilege of making a decision to turn away from a life that is beneath the standard that God has set for you and return to the state of existence where you function in fellowship with God each day of your life.

Dr John R. Adolph

WEEK 1: Make a U-Turn and Keep Straight

Day 1

God's Word For You Today: IF AND ONLY IF

<u>Our Scripture</u>
If my people, which are called by my name, shall humble themselves, and pray, and seek my face, and turn from their wicked ways; then will I hear from heaven, and will forgive their sin, and will heal their land (2 Chron. 7:14, KJV).

<u>Our Simple Lesson</u>
Not long ago, I was traveling in the wrong direction as I sought to find a location in the busy metropolis of Houston to perform a wedding. To make matters worse, traffic was horrible, and I was running late. Of course, I was using my GPS system when, all of a sudden, the subtle, smooth voice of my systemic director informed me to make a U-turn ahead. The area did not look familiar, so I kept going in the wrong direction. Finally, common sense kicked in, and I had a talk with myself, and it went like this, "if you want to get to where you are trying to go, turn around and go the other direction."

Repentance is about making U-turns. It means to halt traveling in the wrong direction and head in the right direction. When Solomon writes to Israel, he reminds them that traveling in the wrong direction never pays big dividends. So he reminds them what to do should they ever find themselves in such a predicament. He says, "If (and only if) my people….would turn from their wicked ways…" It was a nice way of saying if you ever hit a rough spot, it will only get better if and only if you make a U-turn.

<u>Our Serious Need To Change</u>
Take a sincere look at your current walk with God. Since none of us are perfect, find a personal area of your life that is flawed and needs some serious attention. Now, with this in mind, know this: it will only get better if and only if you stop what you are doing, make a U-turn, and go in a new direction.

<u>Our Sincere Petition</u>
Lord, there are some changes I need to make, and I know it. There are areas of my life that require surrender and repentance. I know the choice is mine and my humble request of You right now is to give me the strength to empower my decision so that what I do honors You and blesses me. In The Name of Jesus, Amen

WEEK 1: Make a U-Turn and Keep Straight

Day 2

God's Word For You Today: THIS IS A VERY PERSONAL MATTER

Our Scripture
If my people, which are called by my name, shall humble themselves, and pray, and seek my face, and turn from their wicked ways; then will I hear from heaven, and will forgive their sin, and will heal their land (2 Chron. 7:14, KJV).

Our Simple Lesson
Not long ago, while watching comedian, Steve Harvey, host the Family Feud, I took particular interest in the subject matter at hand, "Things that are personal to you." It was funny and hilarious, at best. There were things listed, like my wallet, my Instagram account password, passcodes, and my toothbrush. But the one that I thought was the most personal was one that wasn't on the board. It was personal decisions that were made.

You know, there are some decisions that you make that impact your life, that are purely personal. When Solomon writes these words, "If my people, which are called by my name," he's talking to a group of people, each of those people have to make up their minds for themselves. When the subject of repentance arises, remember this: it's always personal.

Our Serious Need To Change
Take a moment and ask yourself, "What decisions do I need to make right now for God that would impact my life in a positive way forever?" These decisions are there because you need to make them, and no one else will make them for you.

Our Sincere Petition
Lord, God, if there was ever a time I needed You to help me, it's in matters like these. There are times when I know what I should be doing, and I don't do it. There are times, O God, when I personally struggle with making the right decision. Empower me today, and I promise to obey You like never before because it's my sincere desire to please You.

In The Name of Jesus, Amen.

WEEK 1: Make a U-Turn and Keep Straight
Day 3

God's Word For You Today: THERE'S ONE PRAYER GOD ALWAYS ACCEPTS

Our Scripture
If my people, which are called by my name, shall humble themselves, and pray, and seek my face, and turn from their wicked ways; then will I hear from heaven, and will forgive their sin, and will heal their land (2 Chron. 7:14, KJV).

Our Simple Lesson
There is a misconception about prayer that's circling around the Christian church these days. There are those who think that God answers every prayer the same way. This is just not true. Here's the great misconception. God does hear every prayer; however, He does not respond to every prayer the same. Some prayers are prayed that just get God's attention. One of those prayers, is a prayer that's prayed in humility. Humility strikes the heart of God and causes Him to respond to those prayers that are prayed containing it. When Solomon writes these words, "If my people, which are called by my name, shall humble themselves," humility comes before the petition that's given, and it pulls the heart of God to respond.

Our Serious Need To Change
If you feel like God owes you something, you will never get anything from Him. Humble yourself and realize that if God does nothing else for you, He's already done enough.

Our Sincere Petition
O God, my Father, today, I have learned the lesson of humility. It simply says, "Without You, I am absolutely nothing." Thank You, O God, for being my everything, and I praise You even now for a spirit of repentance that exists in my heart.

In The Name of Jesus, Amen.

WEEK 1: Make a U-Turn and Keep Straight
Day 4

God's Word For You Today: OCEAN, ABOUT-FACE

Our Scripture

If my people, which are called by my name, shall humble themselves, and pray, and seek my face, and turn from their wicked ways; then will I hear from heaven, and will forgive their sin, and will heal their land. (2 Chron. 7:14, KJV).

Our Simple Lesson

I was blessed to be a part of the greatest marching band in the whole wide world while attending Texas Southern University, The Ocean of Soul Marching Band, the ninth wonder of the world. I was a tuba player. As a freshman going into school, we had to attend summer band camp, where we learned face commands for the marching unit. Left face, right face, forward march, backward march. But the one that was the most tricky and challenging to perform was the one where we had to turn and go in the other direction. The command was simple, "Ocean, about face!" You know, the Hebrew word "to turn around" is used in 2 Chronicles 7:14. "If my people, which are called by my name, shall humble themselves and pray and seek my face and turn from their wicked ways," that word "turn" is the word that means "about face." If you're expecting anything from God that's going to be great, and you're in a place where you cannot please God, you'll never get what you desire until you repent and turn around.

Our Serious Need To Change

Take a moment and survey the landscape of your own soul. What are some areas that you really need to see serious change in? Whatever those areas are, repent to God and go in the direction He's calling your life to go in. Follow the Lord and He will guide you.

Our Sincere Petition

Spirit of the Living God, allow my footsteps to be ordered by You so that I move in the direction You would have my life to move in. Forgive me for doing anything that has not been pleasing to You. And I pray these petitions in the One name that matters.

In The Name of Jesus, Amen.

WEEK 1: Make a U-Turn and Keep Straight

Day 5

God's Word For You Today: TRUST ME, HEAVEN HAS THE ANSWER

Our Scripture

If my people, which are called by my name, shall humble themselves, and pray, and seek my face, and turn from their wicked ways; then will I hear from heaven, and will forgive their sin, and will heal their land. (2 Chron. 7:14, KJV).

Our Simple Lesson

I grew up in church listening to Christian clichés. I often heard things like, "God is good all the time, and all the time, God is good." I grew up hearing things like, "The Lord will make a way somehow." But one of the clichés, that stuck with me through the years is the one that says, "Earth has no sorrow that Heaven cannot heal." My brothers and sisters, when we read the words in 2 Chron. 7:14, "...then will I hear from Heaven," it should bring joy to your heart because Heaven has nothing that cannot fix what is wrong on Earth.

There are three realms of Heaven. There is the Heaven that we can see. There is the Heaven of the beautiful blue skies, where the stars are. But beyond that Heaven, is a third Heaven, where the very sovereignty, ubiquity, and veracity of God exists. When we hear the words, "...then will I hear from Heaven," it should let you know that God will certainly have the final say.

Our Serious Need To Change

What is it that Heaven has that you sincerely need? The answer to this question will lead you to a life of blessing, favor, and increase. Think about it and make some changes today.

Our Sincere Petition

So, God, I've come now to say thank You for being the Ruler of the Earth, for being the Ruler of the very heated billows of hell, and for being the sovereign Guide and Ruler of Heaven. Thank You, O God, that the last word in our lives always belongs to You.

In The Name of Jesus, Amen.

WEEK 1: Make a U-Turn and Keep Straight
Day 6

God's Word For You Today: GOOD NEWS, THE JUDGE SAYS YOU'RE FREE TO GO

Our Scripture
If my people, which are called by my name, shall humble themselves, and pray, and seek my face, and turn from their wicked ways; then will I hear from heaven, and will forgive their sin, and will heal their land. (2 Chron. 7:14, KJV).

Our Simple Lesson
Imagine for a moment standing before a righteous judge who is now about to give you the verdict for all of the sins you've committed. There is no jury, just a judge. Imagine for a moment that everything you've done in your past, that's been hidden in a secret closet, has now been exposed, every lie that you've ever told, every horrid, horrible thing you've ever done, things that you're even embarrassed to remember, even as you read this moment of devotional study.

Then, all of a sudden, imagine the righteous Judge walking out of the courtroom, returning with another Man in handcuffs. The Judge tells you, "Don't worry about all of your mistakes. You're free to go. The Gentleman, who is in handcuffs, now stands in your place." You then ask the Judge. "Judge, who is this Man?" The Judge remarks, "He's my Son. I told Him about your predicament, and He said to Me, "Father, let Me take their place."

Today, as you have this moment of devotional study, I want you to realize that your sins, through the grace of God, have all been forgiven: forgiven, cast aside, never to be remembered again, deleted, expunged, erased, done away with.

Our Serious Need To Change
Today is a day when you live like you're forgiven, not to repeat the mistakes of your past. That's what repentance really means: to make a complete change for the better.

Our Sincere Petition
Eternal God my Father, thank You for not giving up on me. Thank You for Your forgiveness. It suits my case. Now, strengthen me to live holy in the days to come.

In The Name of Jesus, Amen.

WEEK 1: Make a U-Turn and Keep Straight

Day 7

God's Word For You Today: FORGIVEN, HEALED AND BLESSED

Our Scripture
If my people, which are called by my name, shall humble themselves, and pray, and seek my face, and turn from their wicked ways; then will I hear from heaven, and will forgive their sin, and will heal their land. (2 Chron. 7:14, KJV).

Our Simple Lesson
When you turn from your wicked ways, the blessing, benefit, and bounty of doing so are found when Solomon writes in 2 Chron 7:14. You are going to hear from Heaven, you will have your sins forgiven, and your land will be healed.

There are three words I would like for you to ponder, hold on to, and consider for the rest of the journey we'll take together. Repentance gives you three things: forgiveness, healing, and the blessing of your land and nation. Hold steadfastly to these and know that God will hear the prayer that you pray that's filled with humility.

Our Serious Need To Change
If there was ever a time when there was a real need for a life-changing decision to choose God and seek Him, it is now. In what ways are you sincerely, devoutly seeking God for the things He has for your life that begin with a change in how you see Him? The answer to this question will lead to favor and blessings. The choice is yours.

Our Sincere Petition
Eternal God, my Father, as I seek Your face, as I call upon Your name, as I humble myself, please hear my prayers. Lord, as I turn from my wicked ways and make decisions that yield blessings, my prayer is that You would allow me to hear from You, forgive my sins, and heal my land.

In The Name of Jesus, Amen.

WEEK 1: Make a U-Turn and Keep Straight
Week 1 Conclusion

HIGHER THAN THE TOP
HT3

Life Application
By now, after studying 2 Chronicles 7:14 for the last several days, you have had to come to the realization that God has been better to you than you've been to Him. If the Lord hears your prayers when they are prayed in humility, and if you have made a decision to turn from your wickedness and know what forgiveness feels like, you have had to reach the conclusion that His blessings and favor on your life make you a debtor to Him.

With this in mind, think of ways you could really serve God in a greater capacity in your local church. If you are already serving the Lord, continue doing so, but increase the capacity and the intensity. Serve like you are a debtor. If you are not serving God at all, if you're not actively engaged or participating in ministry at all, use this moment of life application to take your faith higher than the top.

Contact your church. Tell them you are a willing vessel to serve God while time permits and serve the Lord like He is your God, He is your Lord, and He is your Savior, knowing that one of these days, only what you do for Christ will last.

WEEK 2: The Day God Changed His Mind

Day 1

God's Word For You Today: WHAT YOU DO REALLY MATTERS

Our Scripture
And God saw their works, that they turned from their evil way; and God repented of the evil, that he had said that he would do unto them; and he did it not (Jonah 3:10, KJV).

Our Simple Lesson
I grew up with a mother who was a disciplinarian. She said things one time and expected complete compliance from her children in every way. Her philosophy was simple: if she had to repeat many times before you obeyed her, you were training her and not her training you. She was not having it. I'll never forget the day my mother told us to clean our rooms, and we worked to do so. We had closed the doors to every room and left the den unmade. After all, that was not her request. She came in angry, marched into her room, retrieved a belt, and walked back out. When she opened the doors to our bedrooms, it was spick and span clean from the top to the bottom. Because of our obedience, the wrath, that she once had, shifted and changed immediately. In our study text this week, Jonah reveals the benefits, and blessings of our obedience. When God sees our works and that our works are not the same as they used to be, there is something that happens to the heart of God that causes Him to shift from punishment to blessing. In short, what you do really matters.

Our Serious Need To Change
Never ever think that disobedience goes unpunished, even if met by mercy. The Lord wants your works and your walk in Him to match. He desires obedience, and most importantly, He deserves it.

Our Sincere Petition
O Lord, my Lord, How excellent is thy name in all the Earth. God, hold my hand as I seek to walk and work in a way that causes You to smile upon me and bless me each day. God, bless me today with a spirit of obedience all day long.

In The Name of Jesus, Amen.

WEEK 2: The Day God Changed His Mind
Day 2

God's Word For You Today: WHEN THE PUNISHMENT DOES NOT FIT THE CRIME

Our Scripture
And God saw their works, that they turned from their evil way; and God repented of the evil, that he had said that he would do unto them; and he did it not (Jonah 3:10, KJV).

Our Simple Lesson
Not long ago, I was rushing to get home and was speeding (Don't judge me; just read this devotional with an open mind). After passing by two signs on the freeway that read 65 miles per hour, I slowed from my 90 miles an hour and started to do 65. I put it on cruise control and continued home. Out of the blue, I saw red lights flashing behind me. I was being pulled over with an attitude. I wanted to know why was the officer was stopping me. I got my license and my registration. He tapped on the window and said, "your license, please." I simply acquiesced, and I gave him my credentials. He returned and let me know that he had been following me for over six miles and that I had been speeding, but I made an adjustment. I changed my mind, stopped speeding, and complied with the law. The officer told me he was going to write me a ticket, but because I had made some changes, he would only give me a warning. Today, as you study the book of Jonah 3:10, you see what happens when repentance and turning from a bad way to God's way yields mercy. It's when the punishment really doesn't fit the crime. We should be ticketed. We should be punished, but blessings are always the outcome when you make good adjustments that yield obedience.

Our Serious Need To Change
What change has beckoned your attention right now, where, if you were to be punished for them, the punishment would be severe? You know better, but you just haven't chosen to do better. Here is a challenge for you today. Make the adjustment. Act as if God has been following you the whole time and giving you mercy so that the punishment doesn't fit the crime.

Our Sincere Petition
Eternal God, my Father, thank You for the adjustments that I have been able to make that literally beckon Your mercy and gives me Your grace. Hold my hand, guide my thoughts, order my footsteps, and help me with decision-making this day.

In The Name of Jesus, Amen.

WEEK 2: The Day God Changed His Mind
Day 3

God's Word For You Today: YOUR EVIL DAYS AND YOUR EVIL WAYS

Our Scripture
And God saw their works, that they turned from their evil way; and God repented of the evil, that he had said that he would do unto them; and he did it not (Jonah 3:10, KJV).

Our Simple Lesson
All too often, you spend your time pointing fingers at the sins and mistakes of others. Today's devotional lesson is not about the sins and mishaps of your neighbors, your friends, or people in your family. It's to make you take an introspective look at who you really, really are. Wait! This is not just about your past; it's also about your present. There are times that your evil days and your evil ways should cost you, but when you make the necessary changes, the grace of God meets you in places where the mercy of God can find you, where you know in your heart you deserve the punishment, but God lets you off the hook. He doesn't let you off for free. He only pardons you because you've decided to turn from what was wrong and go in the direction that is right. It's purely repentance at its best.

Our Serious Need To Change
Considering your mistakes always brings you shame and embarrassment. This morning, as you take a moment to study, as you spend this moment of devotional time with God, simply whisper these words to God: "I'm sorry."

Our Sincere Petition
Eternal God, my Father, I realize that my evil days and evil ways should have cost me, but for whatever reason, You have given me the grace that suits my case and the mercy that I sincerely need today. I thank you for both.

In The Name of Jesus, Amen.

WEEK 2: The Day God Changed His Mind
Day 4

God's Word For You Today: HE DID NOT HAVE TO DO IT, BUT HE DID

Our Scripture
And God saw their works, that they turned from their evil way; and God repented of the evil, that he had said that he would do unto them; and he did it not (Jonah 3:10, KJV).

Our Simple Lesson
There are times in your life when you should look at the grace of God and conclude that He didn't have to do it, but He did. He didn't have to bless you. He didn't have to keep you. He didn't have to die to save you. He didn't have to be so sweet to you. The truth is, God has been better to you than you have been to Him.

When you examine Jonah 3:10, the conclusion must be the same. God has been gracious to you when you have not always been obedient and have not always done what He's commissioned you to do, but because of His grace and His love, He lets you make it.

The backbone of today's lesson encourages you to believe and entreats you to embrace the fact that the change you have made toward God only comes from a grace He gives you that you cannot deny. In short, God has been good.

Our Serious Need To Change
Have you reached the place in your walk with the Lord where you really come to grips with the fact that God's grace keeps letting you make it, and the kindness of that grace makes you want to make changes? God loves you mercifully until you change your mind. He often makes room for you to grow into a place where your stupidity becomes humility. I hope and pray that He's done that for you and that your changes to the positive and repentance to God are imminent.

Our Sincere Petition
God, thank You for not giving me what we I truly deserve. Thank You for the mercy You've given me that I know I do not deserve. Give me the time, O God, needed to grow to a place of repentance where my mind shifts and my destiny changes for the better.

In The Name of Jesus, Amen.

WEEK 2: The Day God Changed His Mind
Day 5

God's Word For You Today: SOME THINGS DO CHANGE

Our Scripture
And God saw their works, that they turned from their evil way; and God repented of the evil, that he had said that he would do unto them; and he did it not (Jonah 3:10, KJV).

Our Simple Lesson
The worst comment anyone could ever make to you is to say, "You haven't changed one bit." The prayer is to always have positive change. That I'm taller, that my skin is clearer, that my walk is a little straighter or better. To remain the same is not just an idea of spiritual apathy but the idea that suggests that there's been no progress made.

Today, as you consider Jonah 3:10, it's clear that some things do change. Attitudes change, and when attitudes change, altitudes change. And when altitudes change, outcomes change. And when the outcome changes, destiny changes. Change is inevitable, but in many instances, it should be intentional.

Our Serious Need To Change
Today is a day that God has prescribed time for you to make some intentional changes. Take a moment and consider those changes you seriously need to make, and without hesitation or reservation, make them. It's repentance at its finest.

Our Sincere Petition
Today, God, I take the time to say to You that anything that is not like You in my life, I want to get rid of it. I desire a closer walk with You, so give me the strength to repent and the faith to stay the course.

In The Name of Jesus, Amen

WEEK 2: The Day God Changed His Mind
Day 6

God's Word For You Today: WHEN YOU CHANGED YOURS, HE CHANGED HIS

Our Scripture
And God saw their works, that they turned from their evil way; and God repented of the evil, that he had said that he would do unto them; and he did it not (Jonah 3:10, KJV).

Our Simple Lesson
As we study Jonah 3:10 this week, something shocking is revealed in the "B" clause of the verse. Read it carefully. It reads like this, "And God repented of the evil that He had said that He would do unto them." Did you catch it? God repented. We serve a God that literally looks upon us and repents. The idea of repenting here suggests that God changed His mind, that God was going to do one thing but shifted His mind to do something else instead. What was it that made God change His mind? It was the actions, the attitudes, the works, and the acceptance of His love toward the people of Nineveh that made God say, "I won't destroy them. I will not punish them because they have made some necessary changes."

The joy in today's study is that when you repent and change, God changes towards you. Your repentance and changes do not go unnoticed, and the good news is that they don't go unblessed.

Our Serious Need To Change
Today, God yearns to bless you. Oftentimes, while you're waiting for the blessing to come, God is waiting for the moment to bless you. What's blocking your blessing? There is a need to repent and make changes where you turn your life towards God and continue moving in that direction.

Our Sincere Petition
Eternal God, my Father, thank You, even now, for the space to change, for the strength to change, and for the wherewithal to do so. Today, O God, I make changes in my life that I know will cause You to smile upon me. Bless me and keep me, the day long is my prayer.

In The Name of Jesus, Amen.

WEEK 2: The Day God Changed His Mind

Day 7

God's Word For You Today: HE DID NOT DO IT

Our Scripture
And God saw their works, that they turned from their evil way; and God repented of the evil, that he had said that he would do unto them; and he did it not (Jonah 3:10, KJV).

Our Simple Lesson
There are times that you thank God for the things He has done and those that He did not do. To do such is proper. If you can thank a man for opening a door for you or a kind lady for refilling a tea glass that's sitting on your table, certainly you can thank God for waking you up this morning, for starting you on your way, for life, health, strength, and for all of the many blessings He bestows. But this should not be the only gratitude extended to the God you serve. There are times you should begin thanking God for things He did not do. The last words of Jonah 3:10 read like this, "...and He did it not." When was the last time you took a moment to thank God for the things He did not do? He did not punish you. He did not let you die. He did not hold your past against you, when you made your last mistake. There were so many things that God did not do that should make you say, "Thank You, Jesus and to God be the glory."

Our Serious Need To Change
Just because God didn't punish you does not mean it went unnoticed. Today, I want you to look sincerely and devoutly at your human existence on Earth and all of the things God chose not to do, only to conclude that you owe Him more now than you've ever owed Him before. Make the changes that cause the blessing and move forward.

Our Sincere Petition
Today, O God, gratitude is extended to You from my heart for the things You chose not to do for me. For the doors You left closed, for the ways you didn't make, for the times You didn't fix what was broken. Today, I say thank You. Today, Lord God, I know even now that repentance is what I sincerely need to offer You.

In The Name of Jesus, Amen.

WEEK 2: The Day God Changed His Mind
Week 2 Conclusion

HIGHER THAN THE TOP
HT3

Life Application

You've spent an entire week studying Jonah 3:10. In the root of this passage, the fruit that comes from it is the blessing of one man who has been exposed to God's goodness. He will share his testimony and the good news of the grace of God with people he had every right not to like. Here is a life application moment for you today: when was the last time you shared anything good with a person who was not fond of you? Of course, people like this do exist. Of course, there are people who may not have your best interest at heart. But maybe the reason why they're still in the same predicament and in the same place is because you've withheld the good news of God's grace towards them. You should make it your business this week to do something that would take your faith higher than the top. Send them a note, a text message, a card, or maybe even a phone call that simply says God loved You when you were not lovable. God does the same thing for everyone, and there is nothing like the grace and love of God.

WEEK 3: Change Your Mind About Me

Day 1

God's Word For You Today: I'VE GOT A QUESTION FOR YOU

Our Scripture
While the Pharisees were gathered together, Jesus asked them, saying, What think ye of Christ? Whose Son is he? They say unto him, The Son of David (St. Matthew 22:41-42, KJV).

Our Simple Lesson
Not long ago, while reading some social media posts on Instagram, I stumbled across some comments about Jesus Christ that were horrid, hateful, and heinous, to say the least. I had never read anything so negative on a social post in all my life. The gentleman who made the post said that Jesus was a hypocrite, a counterfeit, a pretender, that He was not God in the flesh, that He was just some Jewish revolutionary whose mission had gone belly up and ended up dying a horrible death at the cross.

The question that looms to be answered this week in your study presses you to come to grips with whether you believe. Here's the question in Matthew 22:41-42, "What think ye of Christ? Whose Son is he?" The answer to this question holds Heaven and hell within its boundaries. The right answer yields golden streets. The wrong answer puts you in torment and flames throughout all eternity.

Our Serious Need To Change
What is your real answer to the question listed above? What do you think about Jesus? Is He really the Christ? Is He really the one who promised to save you from your sins? Is He really your personal Lord and Savior? The answer to this question holds everything within its boundaries. No one can answer it for you but you.

Our Sincere Petition
So, Lord, teach me to see You for who You really are each and every day. Guide me and lead me in these thoughts. Reveal Yourself to me in unique ways, O God, that would cause me to know You in ways like I've never known You before. For in my heart, You are Lord and Christ of this world and the world to come.

In The Name of Jesus, Amen.

WEEK 3: Change Your Mind About Me
Day 2

God's Word For You Today: THE BLESSING OF A CHEAT SHEET

Our Scripture
While the Pharisees were gathered together, Jesus asked them, Saying, What think ye of Christ? Whose son is he? They say unto him, The Son of David (St. Matthew 22:41-42, KJV).

Our Simple Lesson
While in the fifth grade, Mr. Dugan gave us to take a spelling test that I knew I couldn't pass. It was just too much. The words were too broad; the study was too deep. And to make matters worse, I was ill-prepared. But he did something that day that blessed the entire class incredibly. He introduced something to me that I would hold on to forever. He allowed us to have a cheat sheet. A cheat sheet is a sheet where the answers are on it, and all you have to do is refer back to them to get the correct answers on a test.

Jesus, in Matthew 22, gives you a proverbial cheat sheet, if you will. He allows you to look back over the span of His life that has been chronicled, only to realize that He is indeed God made manifest. Jesus is indeed the Christ, Son of the living God, and He is indeed the Creator of the cosmos, the Architect and Engineer of the universe, and the Maker and Creator of all humankind. Today, the blessing is to know that He is who the Bible says He is.

Our Serious Need To Change
How you see Jesus will largely depend on what you have learned about Him through personal experience, literature, studying, and reading the Bible through encounters and testimonies of those who have lived for Him in the past.

Our Sincere Petition
Lord, if there was only one request I would make of You today, it would be this: Help me to know You. Help me to get to know You in greater, more magnificent ways. Because the more I know about You, the more I yearn to know who You really are, what You really are, and how much You've really blessed me.

In The Name of Jesus, Amen

WEEK 3: Change Your Mind About Me
Day 3

God's Word For You Today: SO CLOSE, BUT YET SO FAR

Our Scripture
While the Pharisees were gathered together, Jesus asked them, Saying, What think ye of Christ? Whose son is he? They say unto him, The son of David (St. Matthew 22:41-42, KJV).

Our Simple Lesson
Did you know that there will be people going to hell from pews in a church? It's going to happen because we are so close, but yet so far. To sit on a pew does not make you a Christian; no more than sitting in your garage will make you an automobile. There must be a shift and a change toward Jesus that says, "I have repented. My life will no longer be the same. And though I am not perfect, I thank God I'm not what I used to be."

Today, when you look at these religious leaders in Matthew 22:41-42, the Pharisees are mentioned by name. They are part of the Jewish community that cares deeply about the outward keeping of the law. Their sincerity and commitment are excellent. The problem is they're so close, but yet they're so far. They're far from grace, perfection, mercy, and, in this passage, far from Jesus.

Being far from Jesus is always a negative, bad thing, but being close to him says, "His forgiveness has made room for me, and my repentance and my change have made things for the better."

Our Serious Need To Change
Are there any people who you know of that when you look at them you say ,"Ah, look at their sins?" Today is a day when I want you to look at your sins and begin to say to yourself, "I refuse to let anything keep me from being close to God who I sincerely love and seek to serve."

Our Sincere Petition
And so, God, today as I survey the landscape of my soul, please remove anything from me that would keep me from You because I desire to be closer to You more than I've ever been before in my life.

In The Name of Jesus, Amen.

WEEK 3: Change Your Mind About Me
Day 4

God's Word For You Today: HE'S JUST THE SON OF GOD RIGHT?

Our Scripture
While the Pharisees were gathered together, Jesus asked them, saying, What think ye of Christ? whose son is he? They say unto him, The son of David (St. Matthew 22:41-42, KJV).

Our Simple Lesson
There are two questions listed in Matthew 22: 41-42 that beckons to be answered by everyone. "What think ye of Christ?" And the second question, "Whose Son is He?" Many people say, "He's just the Son of God, right?" But the truth of the matter is not many know what that actually means. This idea of the Son of God is a real poignant - pointed picture of God in human flesh. Not just an offspring or an offshoot of God, but to be from God to the place where the very essence of who God is exists in that individual. Like a drop of water from the Gulf of Mexico reveals what the essence of the Gulf is like, the son of God reveals to you what the character of God is like. For the Son of God reveals to you the character of God, the person of God, the love of God, the power of God, the strength of God, and the very essence of who God is. With this in mind, Jesus is really asking all of us, "Do you believe that I'm Emmanuel? Do you believe that I'm God wrapped in a body?" For the Christian, the answer is an absolute yes!

Our Serious Need To Change
At what point did you really begin to realize that Jesus was indeed God? If your answer is, "I'm not there yet," then my prayer for you is to keep studying until you realize that if Jesus was not God, He is the greatest counterfeit you've ever seen. But if you have received this revelation that only God could calm a raging sea. That only God could heal a man who was sick and blind. That only God could be resurrected after being dead three days. Then take that revelation and live it to the fullest. And if anything keeps you from serving this God, relinquish it, let it go, and walk with God with all your might and faith.

Our Sincere Petition
God, I, too, share sonship in the Father, but my sonship is not like Yours. You are God wrapped in the body, and I am a son by way of adoption. You have chosen to be with me like an adoptive parent would choose a child to be his own. Thank You for choosing me, even before I had an idea of choosing You, and thank You for knowing I would choose You because, after all, You've chosen me. In The Name of Jesus, Amen

WEEK 3: Change Your Mind About Me
Day 5

God's Word For You Today: YOU'VE GOT THE RIGHT ONE

Our Scripture
While the Pharisees were gathered together, Jesus asked them, Saying, What think ye of Christ? whose son is he? They say unto him, The son of David (St. Matthew 22:41-42, KJV).

Our Simple Lesson
Ray Charles Robinson was one of the greatest vocalists and musicians of our age. He rocked audiences with his music, literally, around the world. One of his famed hits was entitled "You've Got The Right One." In your lesson today and your study passage this week, you see Jesus in conversation, dialog, and discourse with some religious leaders called Pharisees. They only care about the outward keeping of the law, and as far as they're concerned, Jesus is no more than some Jewish man born in the poor town of Nazareth who's come from nowhere and is headed nowhere.

Yet, my brothers and sisters, Jesus is indeed the right One. He is the chosen One. He is the only One who can save you from your sins. They missed their window of repentance because they had the right One and did not know it.

Our Serious Need To Change
Here is a pointed, powerful query that you should answer. How do you see Christ? Is He the right one? Is He the one who saves, heals, mends, delivers, and redeems you? If so, you're on the right track. If not, you should get to know Him today.

Our Sincere Petition
God, I thank You for being the only one who qualifies to be the right One in my life. No one else can save but You, no one else can heal like You, and no one else redeems like You. Thank you for saving me.

In The Name of Jesus, Amen.

WEEK 3: Change Your Mind About Me

Day 6

God's Word For You Today: THERE'S NOBODY QUITE LIKE HIM

Our Scripture
While the Pharisees were gathered together, Jesus asked them, Saying, What think ye of Christ? whose son is he? They say unto him, The son of David (St. Matthew 22:41-42, KJV).

Our Simple Lesson
Not long ago, I rushed into the office to catch up on some work that I had gotten behind on. I arrived early in the morning, before daybreak, so that I could work without interruption. As soon as I took my seat, the telephone began ringing. The sun hadn't even risen yet. "Who's calling the church at this hour?" I asked myself. I hurriedly picked up the phone, and a young female asked, "Are you the pastor?" I answered reluctantly, "yes, I am." She said to me, "I have a question for you." She said, "my husband has just returned from prison. He was a Christian; however, he returned as a Muslim." She said, "my husband told me we should not worship the Lord Jesus. We should not pray in His name. We should not attend church regularly. That Jesus is just like all the other religious leaders in our past. But what do you say?" I pushed my chair back from my desk and told the young lady these words: "There is nobody in Heaven, or on Earth, or for that matter, in hell, quite like Him." When the Pharisees confront Jesus, he asks them, "What think ye of Christ? Whose son is he?" The real answer is, "There is nobody like me for you," says the Lord.

Our Serious Need To Change
So, when you look at Jesus Christ, who is He for you? The real answer to this question changes everything. It leads to repentance when you know Him as a Savior, Lord, Redeemer, and Bishop of your soul.

Our Sincere Petition
Eternal God, my Father, it is at this moment that I realize more about You than I've ever known before. You are not just some good man. You are the God, man. You are not just some man who appeared. You are the man who was wrapped in a fleshly body and called Emmanuel, God with us. Thank You for being my Savior and my Lord.

In The Name of Jesus, Amen.

WEEK 3: Change Your Mind About Me
Day 7

God's Word For You Today: EVERYTHING CHANGES WHEN YOU CHANGE YOUR MIND ABOUT HIM

Our Scripture
While the Pharisees were gathered together, Jesus asked them, saying, What think ye of Christ? whose son is he? They say unto him, The son of David (St. Matthew 22:41-42, KJV).

Our Simple Lesson
Everything in your life changes for the better when you change your mind about Jesus Christ. It is not until you change your mind about Him that you see your sin and need to repent. It is not until you change your mind about Him that you realize that God has a plan for your life on Earth. It is not until you change your mind about Him that you trust Him to be a doctor, a friend, a leader, and the guide of your human existence on the planet.

The real lesson today is sometimes religion can block your view of who Jesus really is. Don't let that happen to you. It is not about religion. It's about a relationship with God through His marvelous, magnificent Son, our Messiah, Jesus Christ.

Our Serious Need To Change
What is your current mindset towards God? How do you really see Jesus Christ? Whose Son is He? Answer these questions, change your mind about Him, and everything in your life is going to change for the better and for the greater.

Our Sincere Petition
Spirit of the Living God, rest upon me now and help me to see You the way I should see You, as one that I can trust in, lean on, depend on, rely on, and look to for not just some things but for everything.

In The Name of Jesus, Amen.

WEEK 3: Change Your Mind About Me
Week 3 Conclusion

HIGHER THAN THE TOP
HT3

Life Application

Never forget this: how you see Him is how you will ultimately treat Him. If you see the Lord as a weekend lover that you stop by to visit every Sunday morning for a few moments and leave, then wait until next weekend to see Him again, that's exactly how you would treat Him. But if you see Him as a merciful master, a loving, kind God, a Lord who looks after your every need, then you will treat Him like you love Him every day. In our church family, there are opportunities made for you to show that love for God in your servitude to others. With this in mind, I would like for you to discover your spiritual gifts. Contact your local church and inform them that you would like to know what your spiritual gifts are. Once you discover what your gifts are, I want you to start using those gifts for God's glory and the good of others. If your gift is administration, then locate a place of service in the body of Christ that uses your gift. If your gift is hospitality, then find a place for your hands to help as it pertains to being hospitable. If you are not using your gifts for God's glory, you should pause, change your mind about Him, and unite with us so that your hands can be His. It is repentance at its best when you change your mind about Him, not just in your mindset but in your actions.

WEEK 4: Citizenship Really Matters

Day 1

God's Word For You Today: THE FIRST WORDS ALWAYS MEAN THE MOST

Our Scripture
From that time Jesus began to preach, and to say, "Repent: for the Kingdom of heaven is at hand" (St. Matthew 4:17, KJV).

Our Simple Lesson
The first words that my daughter ever spoke were the words "da-da." I'm sure her mother will read this devotional lesson and completely disagree, but I'll never forget them. It's because they were the first words that she ever uttered. When we read the Constitution of the United States of America, the greatest country in the known world, the first words that are written are "we the people." They are powerful words, pointed words. They are words that give freedom, justice, and rights to the people of our country.

When we read the very first word that Jesus Christ spoke regarding His Kingdom on Earth, it is the word "repent." It translates as "change your mind." You must think differently. It means turning from the direction you are headed in to a brand-new direction.

Our Serious Need To Change
When you start talking about changing your mind, you start talking about changing your destiny. When you start dealing with the fact that you need to change your destiny, a change of mind will change your direction. That's what repentance is really all about: a change of mind that changes your direction forever.

Our Sincere Petition
O Lord my God, as I whisper these sacred supplications and pleas to You, my heart says this: If there is any place in my life that I need to change, give me the strength to do it today. My mind is ready for change. My spirit is ready for change. My heart is prepared for change.

In The Name of Jesus, Amen.

WEEK 4: Citizenship Really Matters

Day 2

God's Word For You Today: THERE'S A NEW KING IN TOWN

Our Scripture
From that time Jesus began to preach, and to say, "Repent: for the Kingdom of heaven is at hand" (St. Matthew 4:17, KJV).

Our Simple Lesson
In your Scripture lesson this week, you find the words of Jesus recorded that say, "repent, for the kingdom of Heaven is at hand." What does He mean by this statement? Here is the answer. Jesus is saying, "listen up, guys, there's a new king in town, and it's Me." In this case, the word "repent" literally means to change kings. To leave one king for another. It's intense, but it's straightforward. You've served one king long enough. There's a new King. This King is one like you've never seen, a King whose boundary is from everlasting to everlasting. A King whose power and ability is limitless. A King whose throne is eternal, not temporal. A King who would die to fight for you so that you might have a life to live. A King whose citizens are part of His Commonwealth, and the blessing of that King will last forever in His people.

Our Serious Need To Change
If you are a part of God's Kingdom on Earth and Jesus is your King, you should rejoice forevermore, for you are blessed and favored, not just by people, but by your King.

Our Sincere Petition
Thank You, O God, for my citizenship in Your country. I may be flawed. I may not be perfect. I may even have shortcomings that I'm trying to overcome. But I do know this: You are my King. I belong to You, and You belong to me.

In The Name of Jesus, Amen.

WEEK 4: Citizenship Really Matters
Day 3

God's Word For You Today: IT'S OUT WITH THE OLD AND IN WITH THE NEW

Our Scripture
From that time Jesus began to preach, and to say, "Repent: for the Kingdom of heaven is at hand" (St. Matthew 4:17, KJV).

Our Simple Lesson
If you're like most people, you love new things, like a new hairdo, new shoes, new clothes, and maybe even a new car. And if you're fortunate, a new house. We love new things; repentance suggests a new direction for your life. It says that you can easily say these words now that you're following Jesus Christ. "It's out with the old and in with the new."

Whenever you begin to walk with God, you will encounter new things: a new belief system, a new faith system, a new currency system, a new way of living, a new way of giving, a new way of existing. And when the new comes, it's out with the old because the new is here and it is not going anywhere.

Our Serious Need To Change
If you're walking with the Lord and holding on to the old, you're doing the Kingdom a great disservice. If you're trying to follow Jesus but hanging on to your perpetual past, you're doing yourself a disservice. Let go of what's old and embrace what's new. The Bible says, "Therefore, if any man be in Christ, he is a new creature." You are new in Christ, so embrace it.

Our Sincere Petition
Lord God, my God, how excellent is thy name in all the Earth. As I approach You right now, I accept the fact that I am new in You, that my old things have passed away, and that I am new because of what You have done for me. Thank God for a new way of living, a new way of giving, a new way of existing, and a new way of seeing my life hidden in Jesus Christ.

In The Name of Jesus, Amen.

WEEK 4: Citizenship Really Matters
Day 4

God's Word For You Today: IMMIGRATION REFORM

Our Scripture
From that time Jesus began to preach, and to say, "Repent: for the Kingdom of heaven is at hand" (St. Matthew 4:17, KJV).

Our Simple Lesson
Right now, you hear so much about immigration reform in America. It's because there are people who live in your country illegally. They do not have any mode of citizenship. They want to be a part of the United States of America but haven't quite gone through the proper procedures to become citizens of the country.

When you hear the word "repent," the big idea is really spiritual immigration reform. It's people who desire Kingdom benefits, but to be a part of the Kingdom, you must accept The King. When you hear the word "repent," it's really dealing with Kingdom citizenship, its blessings, its benefits, its perks, its pluses, its laws, its demands, and the King who governs it.

Our Serious Need To Change
If you are living as a believer in Jesus Christ, you are a part of the citizenship of the Kingdom of God on Earth, whose King shall reign forever; whose blessing, bounty, and benefits are not just those that are trapped in time, but those who run faithfully over into the dawning of eternity. You are a part of the King and His Kingdom, and it is something you should always rejoice about.

Our Sincere Petition
And so, I pray today that You will use me as a citizen of Your Kingdom somehow. Let my light shine among men so they might know my King and understand the blessing He is to me through the sacrifice of His cross.

In The Name of Jesus, Amen.

WEEK 4: Citizenship Really Matters
Day 5

God's Word For You Today: LAWS OF THE KINGDOM OF GOD

Our Scripture
From that time Jesus began to preach, and to say, "Repent: for the Kingdom of heaven is at hand" (St. Matthew 4:17, KJV).

Our Simple Lesson
Any land that you call home has laws that govern the territory. If you live in Texas, you have Texas laws. If you live in Las Vegas, you have Nevada laws. If you live in California, you have California laws. These states are sovereign states, and so it is with the Kingdom of God. It is a sovereign empire governed by one holy King who is above all, whose name is Jesus Christ.

As a Christian, you are a part of the Kingdom of God on Earth, and there are laws that govern your Kingdom. Four Laws: Law number one is the law of love. God defines Himself as such. Without love, it will never be possible to really honor God. Law number two is the law of forgiveness. You forgive others because God has forgiven you. If you don't forgive them, neither will God forgive you. So if you need it, you must release it to others.

Law number three is the law of use. It simply says use what you have for the glory of God and for the good of the God who gave it to you. Law number four is the law of reciprocity. It simply says you sow and reap, that your seed goes into the ground, and that seed yields bountiful, blissful fruit back to you. You sow it because He grows it. You have it because He gave it. These four laws govern the Kingdom.

Our Serious Need To Change
When you look at the four laws, which ones do you struggle with? Here is the news of the day: If you struggle here with any of these, repent. Change today because these laws are non-negotiable.

Our Sincere Petition
Eternal God, my Father, as I live in Your Kingdom on Earth, my prayer today is that You would help me become a law-abiding citizen. Lord, help me follow every law, knowing that You are watching. I desire more than anything to please You.

In The Name of Jesus, Amen.

WEEK 4: Citizenship Really Matters
Day 6

God's Word For You Today: NOT GREEN CARDS, BUT BIRTH CERTIFICATES

Our Scripture
From that time Jesus began to preach, and to say, "Repent: for the Kingdom of heaven is at hand" (St. Matthew 4:17, KJV).

Our Simple Lesson
In America, there are numerous ways of becoming a legal citizen of our country. One way is through naturalization. It's where you go through the legal ramifications of becoming a citizen, and you're issued a green card. Not long ago, while discussing immigration reform and spiritual Kingdom matters with a dear friend, he told me, "What's wrong with the Kingdom of God on Earth is that many believers have green cards but no birth certificates." They have encountered God at church or in some religious way, but they don't believe. Belief, my friends, leads you to the new birth that says, I have been born again.

Our Serious Need To Change
When you look at your life, be honest. Do you see a need to change how you feel about Jesus? Is He a Lord who governs you, a Savior who delivers you, a redeemer who died for you, or is He just some good guy that you've heard about for a long time who's done a few nice things for some people who didn't deserve it? The answer to this question determines your life on Earth and in eternity.

Our Sincere Petition
Lord, today, I thank You for my spiritual birth certificate. I believe that You were born Emmanuel, God with us. I believe You died for my sins and have risen with all power in Your hands. I thank You for your spirit that lives within me, and I plan to serve my King and His Kingdom as long as I have life on Earth.

In The Name of Jesus, Amen.

WEEK 4: Citizenship Really Matters
Day 7

God's Word For You Today: CITIZENSHIP HAS ITS PRIVILEGES

Our Scripture
From that time Jesus began to preach, and to say, "Repent: for the Kingdom of heaven is at hand" (St. Matthew 4:17, KJV).

Our Simple Lesson
Citizenship in many countries has excellent privileges. In America, you have many privileges of just being an American citizen. You have a right to vote. You have a right to use our voice. You have a right to freedom of speech. You have a right to express yourself and be defended by the greatest military on Earth. Like any citizen of America, those who are citizens of the Kingdom of our God have many privileges. Your sins have been wiped away. The joy of the Lord is your strength. The peace of the Lord is yours to possess. The salvation of the Lord is a free gift.

Kingdom citizenship privileges are overwhelming. Every day, you count it a joy and a privilege to serve your King; you have life and life more abundantly. You have a relationship with the King that's personal and intimate. In fact, you can call the King Father, and you are part of a commonwealth, not a democracy, but a theocracy, not capitalism, but a Kingdom. It's because the wealth of the King is common among the citizens. Here's the good news of the day: being a part of God's Kingdom has great benefits both now and forever.

Our Serious Need To Change
Why pass up benefits like these, knowing you will need them today and tomorrow? The benefit package comes to anyone who is a part of the Kingdom of God on Earth. Here's the question: have you met the King? What change do you need to make in order to be a better citizen of the Kingdom? The answers to queries like these will bless you incredibly.

Our Sincere Petition
Lord, today, I thank You for being my King, and I take great joy in being a citizen of the Kingdom of God on Earth, whose national anthem is Amazing Grace; how sweet the sound that saved a wretch like me. Thank You, my King, for being my Governor and My reason for living.

In The Name of Jesus, Amen.

WEEK 4: Citizenship Really Matters
Week 4 Conclusion

HIGHER THAN THE TOP
HT3

Life Application

American citizens pay taxes. You can earn as much money as you would like. Yet when the earnings are finished, there is a debt due that's called a tax debt. Taxes are applicable to everyone who works in America. Like taxes for America, in the Kingdom of God, you don't pay taxes; you give tithes. You don't pay a tithe because there is no bill due. If God sent you an invoice for the services He provides, you couldn't afford to pay it, so you give the Lord a tithe. A tithe means a tenth. It is not equal giving, but it is equal sacrifice. Here on Earth, as a Christian, you are required by God to tithe. Wait! It is essential to understand that tithing, according to the law, was a response to the law, but we tithe under grace. The difference is that tithing, according to law, was to make it an obligatory action, but under grace, it's a voluntarily gift to be given You don't tithe then because you have to, but because you should want to. Look at your life as a believer and as a part of the Church on Earth and ask yourself this question: where does your dime go? If you do not tithe, it is the same as saying, my King and this Kingdom on Earth are not worth 10 cents. If you are tithing, praise the Lord because it's your way of financing the Kingdom of God on Earth.

WEEK 5: It's Do or Die

Day 1

God's Word For You Today: IF YOU DON'T DO IT, YOU'LL DIE

Our Scripture
There were present at that season some that told him of the Galilaeans, whose blood Pilate had mingled with their sacrifices. And Jesus answering said unto them, Suppose ye that these Galilaeans were sinners above all the Galilaeans, because they suffered such things? I tell you, Nay: but, except ye repent, ye shall all likewise perish (St. Luke 13:1-3, KJV).

Our Simple Lesson
I loved playing basketball in my neighborhood. Lakewood Park was a favorite place for me growing up. It was the only time a young man who was portly like me could play the sport. I couldn't dunk. I couldn't touch the rim. I didn't run the court well, but I could shoot. Shooting was a gift for me. I loved the game, Do or Die. It was like the game Horse, but you didn't have that many chances. Here is how the game went. If I shoot before you, you must copy my shot if I hit it. If you don't hit it, you die. You're out of the game.

When it comes to repentance, it's like Do or Die. If you don't do it, you die. Of course, you will die in time, but the death that Christ speaks of is not temporal; it is an eternal one. Repentance is serious business because if you do not repent, you will die. You'll study Luke 13:1-3 for several days. The heart of the verse is simply this: repent or perish.

Our Serious Need To Change
The word "repent" used in this passage is the Greek word "metanoeō." It means after you change your mind. Here's a deep-seated question for you: have you repented yet? Have you changed your mind about Jesus Christ? Are you really looking to walk with Him until the day you die? If you have, you can celebrate that you have done it, which has eternal consequences. And if you have not, what are you waiting for?

Our Sincere Petition
Thank You, O God, for allowing a sinner like me to repent and come to know a God like You. I realize it is not based on my terms but Yours and I have decided to accept Your finished work at the cross as an atonement for my sin.

In The Name of Jesus, Amen.

WEEK 5: It's Do or Die
Day 2

God's Word For You Today: IF YOU DO IT, YOU'LL LIVE

Our Scripture
There were present at that season some that told him of the Galilaeans, whose blood Pilate had mingled with their sacrifices. And Jesus answering said unto them, Suppose ye that these Galilaeans were sinners above all the Galilaeans, because they suffered such things? I tell you, Nay: but, except ye repent, ye shall all likewise perish (St. Luke 13:1-3, KJV).

Our Simple Lesson
I live on the Gulf Coast, and after a few years of fighting it, denying it, and rejecting it, I finally did it. I broke down and bought a windstorm policy for my residential address. We get hit by storms from the Gulf of Mexico, roaring at hundreds of miles an hour. They're called hurricanes, and they do not play. While on the Gulf Coast, I've witnessed eight hurricanes and eight storms that rolled ashore and left ruins and wreckage behind. But I was blessed because I made a decision to do something that blessed me. I bought a windstorm policy. If you do not do it, you will suffer for it. But if you decide to do it, you will always have the necessary insurance coverage. I did it, and I'm glad that I did. When the last hurricane roared ashore, it took land, homes, and furnishings, but I was covered because I had a policy in place.

Repentance in this text is like a divinely inspired insurance policy. If you do it, you'll live. If you don't do it, you'll die.

Our Serious Need To Change
What sense does it make to have insurance to cover you just in case you have a wreck or get hit by a storm and not have a blessed assurance for your soul? Here's the truth: If the Lamb's blood covers you, you are covered. You have done it; you'll live. If you are uncovered and trying to find some coverage that will cover you, then there are no repercussions of eternity for it.

Our Sincere Petition
Thank You, Jesus, for allowing me to have made a decision for You that has changed my life forever. Thank You for the blessed privilege of allowing me to repent. Thank You for allowing me to repent and change my mind while I still have time.

In The Name of Jesus, Amen.

WEEK 5: It's Do or Die

Day 3

God's Word For You Today: TO SAY IT AND NOT DO IT IS DANGEROUS

Our Scripture
There were present at that season some that told him of the Galilaeans, whose blood Pilate had mingled with their sacrifices. And Jesus answering said unto them, Suppose ye that these Galilaeans were sinners above all the Galilaeans, because they suffered such things? I tell you, Nay: but, except ye repent, ye shall all likewise perish (St. Luke 13:1-3, KJV).

Our Simple Lesson
You will hear people often say that talk is cheap, but I want to beg to differ. Words are compelling. Words frame the future. Words become what you simply say. With this in mind, when you hear "repent," it's more than just lip service. This text, Luke 13:1-3, suggests a radical change in a person's mind, where your mind and actions both take the same direction, and you make a U-turn and go the other way. It means to reject one king and that kingdom and to accept another king and a brand-new kingdom. It means to receive Jesus as your personal Lord and Savior.

Our Serious Need To Change
Some people talk about repentance but live in rejection. There are people who say, I've changed my mind about Jesus, but live just the opposite every day, not because of a personal struggle, but because of overwhelmingly displayed disobedience. In what way, in your life right now, do you need to make some serious changes? It's not you waiting on God to make the change; it's God waiting on you to change your mind about Him.

Our Sincere Petition
Lord Jesus, as I look at my life, I see places where I need to make some changes, and I realize that not making them could prove to be dangerous. Give me the courage to make the necessary changes so that my life pleases You every moment of the day.

In The Name of Jesus, Amen.

WEEK 5: It's Do or Die
Day 4

God's Word For You Today: DECISIONS, DECISIONS, DECISIONS

Our Scripture
There were present at that season some that told him of the Galilaeans, whose blood Pilate had mingled with their sacrifices. And Jesus answering said unto them, Suppose ye that these Galilaeans were sinners above all the Galilaeans, because they suffered such things? I tell you, Nay: but, except ye repent, ye shall all likewise perish (St. Luke 13:1-3, KJV).

Our Simple Lesson
Every single day of your life, you make decisions. You decide on what color you're going to wear and what shoes you're going to pair. You decide on what style you'll wear your hair. You make decisions every single day. Did you know that decisions are so powerful for us as human beings that even God doesn't make up our minds for us? It's what makes Luke 13:1-3 so powerful. Jesus tells those who are present to repent or likewise perish. Yet He doesn't change their mind for them. Of course, He could. After all, if He can calm a raging sea, take two fish, and make five barley loaves of bread to feed 5000 people, surely, He could cause people to repent, but He doesn't. He lets them make up their own minds.

Our Serious Need To Change
Today, you have some decisions to make: Whether you will pray or not pray, whether you'll trust God or not trust God, whether you'll depend on Him for what you need, or learn to rely on some other source. You have decisions to make, whether you'll do it right or wrong, good or bad, whether you will build a relationship with the Lord or just remain stuck where you are. The decision is yours. But the most important decision you'll ever make is choosing Jesus and living for Him.

Our Sincere Petition
Oh Lord, today I thank You for allowing me to make up my mind long ago that I would follow Jesus and live for Him. It's a decision I have never regretted. Thank You for receiving me as Your own, and I thank You for being my King of Kings and my Lord of Lords.

In The Name of Jesus, Amen.

WEEK 5: It's Do or Die
Day 5

God's Word For You Today: SOME THINGS GOT TO CHANGE

Our Scripture
There were present at that season some that told him of the Galilaeans, whose blood Pilate had mingled with their sacrifices. And Jesus answering said unto them, Suppose ye that these Galilaeans were sinners above all the Galilaeans, because they suffered such things? I tell you, Nay: but, except ye repent, ye shall all likewise perish (St. Luke 13:1-3, KJV).

Our Simple Lesson
When you look at your life right now, you cannot help but see the need for change in some places. If you're slightly overweight, you may need to change your diet. If you're struggling financially, you may need to change how you handle money. If you're going through a relational challenge, you may need to change the people you are spending your time with. And if you are away from God, you may need to change your mind about Jesus and who the Bible says He is.

When you examine Luke 13:1-3, which you've been looking at all week long, the real gist of today's lesson is this: Change your mind about the Lord. Make a U-turn and come back to Him. There are those of you who have already made up your mind that "I'm going to follow Jesus." For those who have, Praise the Lord, but if you have not, I say that "some things got to change."

Our Serious Need To Change
Changing a tire can be difficult, requiring all kinds of metric tools. Changing your oil can be a trick or two. Changing some things can be hard, but changing your mind is simple. It is just one simple change: from worry to worship, from panicking to prayer, from doubting to belief. You should make that change today and live within its benefits.

Our Sincere Petition
Lord Jesus, help me make the changes I can with my strength. Empower me to work through the changes I cannot do by myself. Thank You today for the changes You've empowered me to make, which have already been a blessing to me. That change for me is making sure I choose You.

In The Name of Jesus, Amen.

WEEK 5: It's Do or Die

Day 6

God's Word For You Today: WHAT DOES IT MEAN TO PERISH?

Our Scripture
There were present at that season some that told him of the Galilaeans, whose blood Pilate had mingled with their sacrifices. And Jesus answering said unto them, Suppose ye that these Galilaeans were sinners above all the Galilaeans, because they suffered such things? I tell you, Nay: but, except ye repent, ye shall all likewise perish (St. Luke 13:1-3, KJV).

Our Simple Lesson
As you study Luke 13:1-3 this week, you must look carefully at the word "perish" used at the end of verse 3. The word "perish" here comes from a Greek word that means not to destroy or to delete or to crush, but it means to eliminate. It was used as a word that would describe something burned in a fire.

Nothing comes in contact with fire and remains the same. In a fire where some things have burned, they come out differently. There are some things that are covered with black soot, but if you wipe the soot away, the object is still there. There are some things that are partially destroyed, where the fire has destroyed pieces and portions but has not consumed all of it. And there are items that are completely destroyed. The fire has burned the object beyond recognition and completely eliminated it. This is what the word "perish" means in Greek. It means to be completely annihilated.

Our Serious Need To Change
Jesus uses this term because it directly references the effect and judgment Hell's fire will have on those who have not repented. Wait! Don't let this frighten you. Because even though there is judgment, there is a way out, like a fire hatch, like an escape patch, like a way to get away from the flames of eternal damnation. It's simply to believe in Him, who was sent from the Father to save you by the birth of the Son, who was stamped by the Holy Spirit and will be here for you in both time and eternity.

Our Sincere Petition
Today, O God, I thank You for saving me from eternal judgment and damnation, as well as from my enemies and myself. Thank You today for life in time and life that is now eternal.

In The Name of Jesus, Amen.

WEEK 5: It's Do or Die

Day 7

God's Word For You Today: MY MIND'S MADE UP, NO TURNING BACK

Our Scripture

There were present at that season some that told him of the Galilaeans, whose blood Pilate had mingled with their sacrifices. And Jesus answering said unto them, Suppose ye that these Galilaeans were sinners above all the Galilaeans, because they suffered such things? I tell you, Nay: but, except ye repent, ye shall all likewise perish (St. Luke 13:1-3, KJV).

Our Simple Lesson

You can learn so much from the lives of those who taught you the Christian faith. Your ancestors, who may sleep now, because they've passed from time into eternity. Many of them taught you how to pray and read the scriptures. They shared their testimonies of faith, endurance, suffering, and overcoming with you.

A lady lived at 4440 Booker Street in Beaumont, Texas. We called her Mother Brown at the Antioch church. She passed away several years ago, and as her body grew weaker and as her mind grew a little dimmer, she would often call for me to come and visit with her. She held my hand on one occasion and said, "My mind's made up. There's no turning back."

This week, we've been studying one verse of Scripture, the passage in Luke 13:1-3, where Jesus literally says to a company of people, repent or perish. It was His way of saying these words: "once you decide, there is no turning back".

Our Serious Need To Change

The most dangerous person in the world is a Christian who lives with a made-up mind. Their faith is strong, their resolve is real, and their commitment and covenant to serve the Lord, both in and out of season, will never change. Here is a poignant, pointed question for you to answer. Is your mind made up yet?

Our Sincere Petition

Lord Jesus, today, I want You to know that my mind is made up regarding You, Your word, the worship that I yield, the service that I give, and the life that I live. My mind is made up, and I am not turning back.

In The Name of Jesus, Amen.

WEEK 5: It's Do or Die
Week 5 Conclusion

HIGHER THAN THE TOP
HT3

Life Application

The faith that you live is the result of a decision that you've already made. That decision impacts your life in every category, including your life as a believer in the congregation of people you unite with called a church. Your church family should know that you're living for the Lord because your mind is made up. Whether you sing or serve as an usher. Whether you're part of a vision team. Whether you serve on the parking lot. Wherever or whatever your service to God, it ought to happen in a way that expresses jubilant joy and purpose that says, "I'm serving, not to receive a plaque or an award," but to hear the God I serve and the King I love to tell me "well done" when life is over.

Here is a critical question regarding your life as a believer on Earth with the Church: has your mind really been changed? Do you really see that you owe God more than you could ever repay Him? Is your mind made up about worship, walking with God, witnessing His goodness, and working for you while you have time? Here is the blessing of this week's study. Your mind is made up. You're not turning back. Jesus has changed your life, and you plan to serve Him forever.

WEEK 6: Thank God, He Gave Me a Chance to Change

Day 1

God's Word For You Today: WE KEEP COMING UP SHORT

Our Scripture
And Zacchaeus stood, and said unto the Lord: Behold, Lord, the half of my goods I give to the poor; and if I have taken any thing from any man by false accusation, I restore him fourfold. And Jesus said unto him, This day is salvation come to this house, forsomuch as he also is a son of Abraham. For the Son of man is come to seek and to save that which was lost (St. Luke 19:8-10, KJV).

Our Simple Lesson
The human condition suggests that we keep coming up short. No matter where you look, you will always find people far from perfect. Clinton came up short with Monica Lewinsky. Tyson came up short against James Buster Douglas. In Super Bowl LIX, the Chiefs came up short against the Eagles. Wherever you look, we just keep coming up short.

This week, as you study repentance in Luke 19:8-10, you will discover a story about a gentleman whose name is Zacchaeus, who was born short, lived short, and at the end of his life was still short. Yet, God found space in His presence for a short man who would dare repent.

Our Serious Need To Change
In what ways do you come up short? Wait, be honest with your answer. It could lead to great resolve. The truth of the matter is that everyone comes up short. Right now, I don't want you to think about the shortcomings of others. I'd like for you to analyze the deficiencies that befall you.

Our Sincere Petition
O God, how excellent is Your name in all the Earth! As I pray my prayer today, I realize that there are many spaces and places in my life where I fall short. Grant me Your mercy, and thank You for giving me the blessed chance to make a change.

In The Name of Jesus, Amen.

WEEK 6: Thank God, He Gave Me a Chance to Change

Day 2

God's Word For You Today: EVEN IF YOU CLIMB A TREE, YOU STILL CAN'T FIX YOUR PROBLEM

Our Scripture
And Zacchaeus stood, and said unto the Lord: Behold, Lord, the half of my goods I give to the poor; and if I have taken anything from any man by false accusation, I restore him fourfold. And Jesus said unto him, This day is salvation come to this house, forsomuch as he also is a son of Abraham. For the Son of man is come to seek and to save that which was lost (St. Luke 19:8-10, KJV).

Our Simple Lesson
We often try to find ways to fix our shortcomings as human beings. We bloat our resumes with beautiful, notable accolades. We often boast of our bank accounts, annuities, or financial prowess so that we can eliminate the human condition of coming up short.

Today, in your lesson, Zacchaeus did something that I found most interesting. He knows that Jesus is coming, so to adjust to his short physical stature, he climbs a tree to see Jesus and to look from a limb. The blessed part about today's story is that at least he wanted to see Jesus badly enough to climb a tree. The tragedy of today's story is that even after climbing a tree, his condition was the same. He was a short man.

Our Serious Need To Change
You cannot fix your condition, only God can. You cannot adjust your being short any more than you can change the color of your skin color or change your DNA makeup. It is what it is. The Scriptures teach us on this wise: "All we, like sheep, have gone astray. All have sinned and come short of the glory of God."

Our Sincere Petition
Lord, if there was ever a time in this life I needed you, it is right now. I've tried fixing myself, and each time I make an endeavor at self-repair, something else breaks. So right now, I give my life to You. After all, You made me, and I am best in Your hands.

In The Name of Jesus, Amen.

WEEK 6: Thank God, He Gave Me a Chance to Change
Day 3

God's Word For You Today: HE KNOWS YOUR SINS BUT CALLS YOU BY YOUR NAME

Our Scripture
And Zacchaeus stood, and said unto the Lord: Behold, Lord, the half of my goods I give to the poor; and if I have taken anything from any man by false accusation, I restore him fourfold. And Jesus said unto him, This day is salvation come to this house, forsomuch as he also is a son of Abraham. For the Son of man is come to seek and to save that which was lost (St. Luke 19:8-10, KJV).

Our Simple Lesson
We live in a generation that loves pointing fingers at the flaws of others. I contend that the reason this keeps happening is because it's easier for us to discuss where others fall short than it is for us to confront our shortcomings.

In today's lesson, Zacchaeus is this man's name, and his sins are many. You see, he is a tax collector. He is considered one of the worst sinners of first century Judaism. He is known for lying, stealing, and being destructive. He works on the government's behalf to extort and take advantage of his own people. He is the worst of sinners, and Jesus is aware of this. But the shout of today's lesson is this: Jesus knows his sins, but He calls him by his name. Zacchaeus is his name. His sins are many, but the Lord doesn't refer to any of them because he has a name in God's heart.

Our Serious Need To Change
How would it make you feel to know that God knows every single one of your sins? Sins of the mind, that's things you just thought about; sins of the flesh that you have actually committed. He even knows about your private mishaps that were done in the dark that have never been brought into the light. He knows all of them. But when God gives you a chance to change, remember this: He doesn't think about your sins. He's already died for those. He calls you by your name.

Our Sincere Petition
Thank You, O God, today, for knowing my condition but loving me enough to call me by my name. Today, O God, I seek to get to know You better than I've ever known You before, for if You can call me by my name, I can bow my knee to Yours.

In The Name of Jesus, Amen.

WEEK 6: Thank God, He Gave Me a Chance to Change
Day 4

God's Word For You Today: GOD'S LOVE CHANGES EVERYTHING

Our Scripture
And Zacchaeus stood, and said unto the Lord: Behold, Lord, the half of my goods I give to the poor; and if I have taken anything from any man by false accusation, I restore him fourfold. And Jesus said unto him, This day is salvation come to this house, forsomuch as he also is a son of Abraham. For the Son of man is come to seek and to save that which was lost (St. Luke 19:8-10, KJV).

Our Simple Lesson
One of the things God uses to pull you towards Him is a radical, undeniable, life-changing encounter with His love. If there is nothing else you've gained or learned by reading this devotional book on repentance, remember this: God loves you! God loves you more than your mind could ever contain, or others could ever explain. His love is permanent, overwhelming, and real.

In our story this week, God loves a tax collector so much that He tells him, "Come down. I'm going to go to your home with you." How dare a Holy Christ go to the home of a practicing sinner Zacchaeus? Yet He does it for one reason: God loves the worst of us because He has the best of grace for the sin that you're in.

Our Serious Need To Change
God loves you so much that He wants His love to change your life. When you really grow in grace, here's what you discover: what you've been looking for and longing for all of your life is a love that is only like the love God gives. You'll never find it in people, places, things, markets, or purchases. You will only find it in the hand and the heart of God.

Our Sincere Petition
Bless your name today, O Lord, is my cry. Thank You for loving me, even in times and seasons when I was unlovable, especially when I didn't love myself. Thank You for showing me what real love is all about in Your actions toward me at the cross.

In The Name of Jesus, Amen.

WEEK 6: Thank God, He Gave Me a Chance to Change
Day 5

God's Word For You Today: I'M SORRY, I WAS WRONG AND I KNOW IT

Our Scripture
And Zacchaeus stood, and said unto the Lord: Behold, Lord, the half of my goods I give to the poor; and if I have taken any thing from any man by false accusation, I restore him fourfold. And Jesus said unto him, This day is salvation come to this house, forsomuch as he also is a son of Abraham. For the Son of man is come to seek and to save that which was lost (St. Luke 19:8-10, KJV).

Our Simple Lesson
As you've looked to gain knowledge and insight regarding repentance from Luke 19:8-10 this week, it should not go without mentioning that the word "repent" is not found in the narrative. It's not in any of the verses where Zacchaeus repented. However, what Zacchaeus does is change his mind about the Lord and the things he's done wrong, so much until Zacchaeus knows he's been a thief and a liar. Rather than be fake or fictitious about it, he says, "Lord, the half of my goods I give to the poor. And if I've taken anything from any man by false accusation, I restore him fourfold." Then, Jesus said, "Today, at this very moment, salvation has come to this house."

Jesus was saying, "Repentance looks good on you, Zacchaeus." On the day that you admit that you're sorry and you change your mind, "God says, "You wear repentance well and it looks good on you too."

Our Serious Need To Change
Have you ever had a moment where the love of God brought you to tears because you knew you were wrong about certain actions, attitudes, and things you have done? Today is a day when your actions are to follow a decision that brings about a sorrow that says, "Lord, I'm sorry for the wrong that I've done, and I knew it."

Our Sincere Petition
Lord, on a good day, I still make mistakes. And on days, O God, when I think I have it all together, I'm still marred because of who I am. Yet I come to You with sincerity, and I say to You right now, I am so sorry for every sin I've ever committed. Thank You for forgiving me and for giving me a chance to change.

In The Name of Jesus, Amen.

WEEK 6: Thank God, He Gave Me a Chance to Change
Day 6

God's Word For You Today: ACTIONS SPEAK LOUDER THAN WORDS

Our Scripture
And Zacchaeus stood, and said unto the Lord: Behold, Lord, the half of my goods I give to the poor; and if I have taken anything from any man by false accusation, I restore him fourfold. And Jesus said unto him, This day is salvation come to this house, forsomuch as he also is a son of Abraham. For the Son of man is come to seek and to save that which was lost (St. Luke 19:8-10, KJV).

Our Simple Lesson
Though resting now with the ancestors, my mother often taught her children lessons that would stay with us for the rest of our lives. Mama would say things to you like, "Everybody that's your color isn't your kind." She would let you know that everything that glitters isn't always gold. My mother would say "everything that feels good to you isn't always good for you." She would say, "Every tub has to sit on its own bottom and every mule has to pull its own load." But the one that sticks with me the most in which I found biblical roots throughout the canon for is this old saying: "Actions speak louder than words." It suggests something more than just lip service. It means that what you say is followed by actions that support what you meant.

In this week's narrative, Zacchaeus is not just talking; he is acting. He's not just saying, "I repent." He is letting you see what repentance looks like on an 85-inch flat-screen LED made by one of our finest producers. Zacchaeus's life says, "This is what repentance looks like."

Our Serious Need To Change
What does your life look like when it comes to repentance? Are you saying it and not doing it? Are you trying to do it and failing at it? Have you made some decisions and said, "You know what, today is a day I'm not only saying it, but I'm also doing it, and I'm living it moment by moment and day by day?" My prayer for you is that the latter is the truth. Live it because it's yours to live.

Our Sincere Petition
Today, O God, I need your strength to live the decisions I have made because I know that my actions in your sight speak louder than the words I could ever declare. Thank you, O God, today for the changes You've already made in my life, and I celebrate those that are yet to come.
In The Name of Jesus, Amen.

WEEK 6: Thank God, He Gave Me a Chance to Change
Day 7

God's Word For You Today: WHEN SHORT PEOPLE MAKE TALL CHANGES

Our Scripture
And Zacchaeus stood, and said unto the Lord: Behold, Lord, the half of my goods I give to the poor; and if I have taken any thing from any man by false accusation, I restore him fourfold. And Jesus said unto him, This day is salvation come to this house, forsomuch as he also is a son of Abraham. For the Son of man is come to seek and to save that which was lost (St. Luke 19:8-10, KJV).

Our Simple Lesson
After studying this narrative all week, it seems easy to conclude that what made Zacchaeus tall in God's eyes was not his physical height but his faith in the Lord, which made him change his mind and do some things differently. With this in mind, short people can make tall decisions.

When the Lord looked at Zacchaeus' decision to reverse his attitude of theft, to give back to those he had taken from, to stop that action and activity, the announcement of salvation and the presence of God came into that house. Today, as you look at Zacchaeus, and his problem of sin and being short, you cannot help but consider your own sins and shortcomings. All of us, like Zacchaeus, keep coming up short. What makes you large in the eyes of the Lord is to make a decision that says, "It's time for a change."

If Zacchaeus made a decision for change, so can you. If he made a decision for what was better that would come from God, so can you. The real question that looms to be answered is this: what on earth are you waiting for?

Our Sincere Petition
Great is the Lord, and He is to be praised greatly. Thank you, O Lord, at this very moment for giving me the right and the wherewithal to make big decisions. Lord; today, as I move from where I am forward, my prayer is that You would give me everything it would take to make big decisions that would yield fruitful outcomes, starting with Your will and desire for my life. Lord, I yield myself to You, and I say whatever You want to do with me; from this moment, I am Yours.

In The Name of Jesus, Amen.

WEEK 6: Thank God, He Gave Me a Chance to Change

Week 6 Conclusion

HIGHER THAN THE TOP
HT3

Life Application

Decisions that are key in your life come when God presents opportunities for you to do things for Him and His Kingdom on Earth. Many Christians are part of local assemblies, who sit each week and do nothing as it pertains to Christian service. Your church is a church that's on the move for God, but it should be moving with your hands, your energy, your effort, your excellence, and your active, vibrant participation. With this in mind, I want to challenge you to make a big decision, to deepen your service, to heighten your faithfulness, by saying to God, "Lord, use my hands, use my heart, use my life, use my entire testimony for the good of others and the glory of God.

For example, at Antioch Missionary Baptist Church in Beaumont, Texas where I'm privileged to Pastor there are opportunities for service in ministry constructs that help us fulfill both our vision and core values like our Youth and Children's V.I.P. Ministry, and our collegiate young adults like our Relentless LU-CRU student organization at Lamar University. We have our Men at the Master's Table Men's Ministry, we have ministries that meet the unique needs of women like FLO (For Ladies Only) and WOP (Women of Purpose). We even offer community based ministries that use the service of volunteers to Feed the Homeless, strengthen our international ties through Global Missions in countries around the world and the list goes on. To be clear, we offer nearly fifty different ministries that help us meet the needs of the total personal at Antioch. My challenge to every member that is connected to our faith family is to become a part of the church's vision by finding a place for your hands and heart to serve God as a difference maker and a trend setter. Make a decision to serve God today. This way when time is over you can earnestly say, may the works that I have done speak for me.

WEEK 7: It's Hot in Here

Day 1

God's Word For You Today: THERE ARE SOME THINGS MONEY CAN'T BUY

Our Scripture
And he said, Nay, father Abraham: but if one went unto them from the dead, they will repent (St. Luke 16:30, KJV).

Our Simple Lesson
You live in a culture pressed by creature comforts; things that cash and credit can buy, things that checks can write. With this in mind, you are surrounded by a country pressed by labels and name-brand items. As a collective group Americans love the larger things in life. In fact, for some people the more expensive your shoes are and the more money you spend on your clothing, the more respect you gain from those in your concentric circle of contact. In short, our current culture is impressed with expensive cars, nice clothes and lots of cash.

However, there is a warning that comes from this week's story that basically lets you know that the currency of Heaven is not the same currency we use on Earth. In short, there are some things that money cannot buy. Money cannot buy a place in Heaven for you. Money cannot buy grace from God on your behalf. Money cannot buy salvation, hope, joy, peace, or even the ability to endure. There are just some things that cash cannot afford.

Our Serious Need To Change
In today's story, we learn the narrative of a rich man and Lazarus. The rich man had all of his magnificent things in time but died without knowing God. The poor man died leaning on the everlasting arms of God and ended up in Abraham's bosom. The good news about the man who was poor was that Lazarus took time to make some changes while he could.

Our Sincere Petition
Lord, if there are any changes that I need to make in my life, give me the strength right now to make them. I want to please You and sincerely make You happy with me. I pray these solemn supplications in the only name that matters.

In The Name of Jesus, Amen.

WEEK 7: It's Hot in Here

Day 2

God's Word For You Today: CONTRARY TO POPULAR OPINION, HELL IS REAL

Our Scripture
And he said, Nay, father Abraham: but if one went unto them from the dead, they will repent (St. Luke 16:30, KJV).

Our Simple Lesson
You live in a culture where everybody who dies goes to Heaven. However, what this passage of study opens the door to, and the truth to, is that if there is a heaven, there is also a hell. Hell is just as real as Heaven. The interesting irony that we have to live with is that most people never mention going to hell. They only want Heaven in the afterlife. There is a rich man in this passage who fares sumptuously, yet he uses what he has to be oppressive to those who are poor, and the end result for that man is hell. He is so concerned about his relatives that still have time. The rich man in hell makes a request for someone who has been to hell to go tell his family and friends that hell is a place of torment. But, the request was denied simply because once it's over, it is over.

Our Serious Need To Change
Have you ever known someone who passed away and doubted whether they believed or not? As you read this devotional, may I suggest that you treat this moment as one that says, "I want those I love to live in Heaven with God and with me." Take a moment and pray for them because God has put them close enough to you for you to sincerely make petitions on their behalf.

Our Sincere Petition
Father, at this moment, I intercede and pray for those I know and love who I want to see, believe in, and follow you. God, You know them, name by name, and You know the ones on my heart. Lord, let their hearts find Your love. Let them encounter Your grace in such a way that they would come to know You through a spirit of repentance.

In The Name of Jesus, Amen.

WEEK 7: It's Hot in Here

Day 3

God's Word For You Today: ONCE IT'S OVER YOU CAN'T GO BACK

Our Scripture
And he said, Nay, father Abraham: but if one went unto them from the dead, they will repent (St. Luke 16:30, KJV).

Our Simple Lesson
Often, people have the most interesting questions for me as a Pastor. One young lady asked one day, "Pastor Adolph, are palm readings true?" I asked her why she made the inquiry. She said that she had been to the city of New Orleans and paid to have her palm read on Bourbon Street. She concluded by telling me that the palm reader said that she would die. I asked her how much the palm reader charged. She said, "$29.99." I told that young lady, "I could have given you that information for free." The Bible said, "It's appointed unto every man once to die and after this the judgment." Oftentimes, you hear people make statements like, "Perhaps I could have a conversation with someone who is from the dead," "Let the dead go and speak," or "Let the dead testify." But I want you to leave this week of study knowing this: once it's over, you cannot go back. We learn that truth from this particular story of the rich man who wants to go and have one from the dead, go to his loved ones, and make an announcement and declaration to warn his loved ones about the reality of the burning inferno of hell. His request is denied. It's a picture-perfect portrait of the fact that once you're over in time, you cannot go back.

Our Serious Need To Change
If there were people near you that you knew needed God, would you be bold enough to tell them the truth about the God that you serve? Or would you just hope they find out through some other means? We no longer treat hell as a burning inferno. We almost treat hell as if it is nonexistent. But the truth of the matter is that some people are going to end up in Heaven by the grace of God, and others will have to face eternal judgment in hell. Today's profound need to change is not letting anyone you know end up in hell without you telling them the truth about Jesus Christ.

Our Sincere Petition
Lord, have mercy on me and thank You for giving me a chance to make changes in my life. The most significant change I've ever made is accepting You as my Lord and Savior. Now, God, do the same for those that I love so that everyone I've seen on Earth will be in Heaven. In The Name of Jesus, Amen.

WEEK 7: It's Hot in Here

Day 4

God's Word For You Today: SOME PEOPLE WILL NEVER CHANGE

Our Scripture
And he said, Nay, father Abraham: but if one went unto them from the dead, they will repent (St. Luke 16:30, KJV).

Our Simple Lesson
There are times that I listen to the testimonies of atheists and why they choose not to believe in God. The citations they make are the most interesting. In my opinion, denying God is an affirmation that He is there because you cannot ignore something that is not present.

As I listened to one atheist not long ago talk about how there is no God, no presence of a deity, and no evidence of one, my mind couldn't help but think about the story that we've been studying this week. The young man with the testimony was wealthy and affluent, magnificent and splendorous in his appearance. He wore gold, diamonds, and a very nice Rolex watch. His clothing was extravagant. I could not help but think about this rich man in Luke 16:30 who made up his mind that his wealth meant more to him that getting to know God.

In short, the rich man in our study passage this week had a chance to change but never did.

Our Serious Need To Change
The wise man knows there is a God. The fool has said in his heart that there is none. Be wise enough to know if there is a shoe, there is a shoemaker. Be wise enough to know that if there is a house, there is a house-maker. And if there is a physical body, there is a physical body maker. And if there's a brain, there's a brain maker. And if there is a life that you live, there is someone who gave it to you who's bigger than you.

Our Sincere Petition
And so, God, I approach You with fear, knowing that You know everything. Lord, I ask even now that you have pity and mercy upon those who have made up in their minds that You do not exist, and Lord, for those who will never change, O, God, I pray, have mercy on their soul.

In The Name of Jesus, Amen.

WEEK 7: It's Hot in Here
Day 5

God's Word For You Today: FIVE THINGS ABOUT HELL YOU SHOULD NEVER FORGET

Our Scripture
And he said, Nay, father Abraham: but if one went unto them from the dead, they will repent (St. Luke 16:30, KJV).

Our Simple Lesson
As you read this particular story of the rich man who never repented and ended up in hell, we need to realize that this one passage of scripture contains radical biblical truth about hell and its reality. Take note of these things.

Reality number one: hell is hot. We know this because the rich man says he is being tormented in the flames. The word "torment" used in the passage means to be ruined or burned. It's horrible because you are consumed with fire but not destroyed. Number two, here's the second reality: You can go to hell and still be alive. Some people think that once you are dead, it's over, but the truth is, the rich man is alive and feels everything. Reality number three: It's painful. The truth is this, hell hurts. The flames were not just hot; they were painful. Reality number four: Hell has no exits. For the rich man in Luke 16 there was no way out. And lastly, hell lasts forever. How long does forever last? Long enough for the sea to touch the sky and for infinity to become beyond. In short, forever last forever.

Our Serious Need To Change
A man once asked me, "Why does God send people to hell if He's so good?" My answer was simple: "God doesn't send anyone to hell. People make a choice to live there." Here is my challenge to you: make a wise choice. Live life like there is a heaven, and you plan to spend eternity there.

Our Sincere Petition
So, God, today I thank You for the salvation You have given me based on your grace. Thank You, O God, for making room near You for a person like me today, for I know it was nothing but Your grace that would spare me from a burning hell.

In The Name of Jesus, Amen.

WEEK 7: It's Hot in Here

Day 6

God's Word For You Today: DEATH IS NOT A THREAT, IT'S A REALITY

Our Scripture
And he said, Nay, father Abraham: but if one went unto them from the dead, they will repent (St. Luke 16:30, KJV).

Our Simple Lesson
Once, while in the gym, I ran into a gentleman who was a very dear friend of mine. His name was Mr. EJ. He stopped me that day with a towel wrapped around his neck and a beautiful gold chain around his neck and said to me, "Reverend, are you still lying to those people at the church?" with a smirk on his face. I answered and said, "What do you mean?" He said to me, "Reverend, we both know there is no heaven and there is no hell. Once life is over, it's just over." I said, "Mr. EJ, let's suppose you're right and I'm wrong. There is no heaven and no hell. What have I lost by loving my neighbor, treating people kindly, and helping those in need?" Then I said, "Mr. EJ, what if I'm right and you're wrong? What if you discover after you die that there really is a God, there really is a heaven, and there really is a hell." I said, "You would lift your eyes in hell." He looked at me and said, "How dare you threaten me with death?" I said, "Sir, death is not a threat. It's a reality. Your eyesight is growing dimmer, your steps are shorter each day as you walk around this track, and right now, you have more time behind you than you have ahead of you." I told him death was a promise and a reality for everyone on the planet.

Our Serious Need To Change
Before you take your last breath, I would give you a word of wisdom, just like I would have given the rich man in Luke 16. Get to know the Lord before it's too late.

Our Sincere Petition
Lord Jesus, thank You for including me in your redemptive plan before time passed. Thank You for making room for me near your cross so that I might come to know You in the pardon of my sins. Oh Lord, thank you for saving me.

In The Name of Jesus, Amen.

WEEK 7: It's Hot in Here
Day 7

God's Word For You Today: IT'S JUST FOR THOSE WHO REFUSE TO CHANGE

Our Scripture
And he said, Nay, father Abraham: but if one went unto them from the dead, they will repent (St. Luke 16:30, KJV).

Our Simple Lesson
In the story you have studied all week long, both men die. More specifically, both the rich man and the poor man die. The reality here is that both men pass away. Death for us on Earth is inevitable. However, one man ends up in Abraham's bosom. A categorical study of scripture reveals that Abraham's bosom was the place a soul would reside before Jesus died on the cross and rose from the dead. It was like Heaven. It was a holding tank for those who loved God. But on the other side of a gulf that separated them were the fiery billows of hell. It was as if both of these realities existed, Heaven and Hell. Notice, however, that hell was not made for us. It was only made for the devil and His angels and for those who simply refused to change.

Our Serious Need To Change
There comes a time when change is not just needed—it's an overwhelming necessity. The word "repent" in this text is the Greek word that means to change your mind before it's too late. To shift your thinking about God, His grace, His goodness, His Son, your life on Earth, and your time in eternity. Make up your mind today about who you will serve.

Our Sincere Petition
Lord Jesus, I am thankful to call You my Savior, My Lord, and my God. Unlike some, my mind is already made up, and I'm never going to change it. If You loved me enough to die for me, I care enough to live for You.

In The Name of Jesus, Amen.

WEEK 7: It's Hot in Here
Week 7 Conclusion

HIGHER THAN THE TOP
HT3

<u>Life Application</u>
It should be the desire of every Christian to live a life on Earth well enough to pass from time and to live in eternity with the voice of God that would welcome that believer home by simply saying, "Servant, well done." It is mine to ensure you understand that you will not hear God say, "Well done," unless you first do well. To make that happen, well done by doing well suggests repentance.

If you are reading this devotional and you are not for certain where you stand with God I want you to repent. Change your mind about your life, your sin, and your need for a Savior. Change your mind about how you see God in the person of Jesus Christ and His church on Earth. Join a local assembly of believers and become a member of a Bible believing, spiritually led church and serve God with everything that you have in your heart. After all, He gave His life so that you could have a lift to live. So, give Him your life while you still have life left.

WEEK 8: He Changed My Life Forever

Day 1

God's Word For You Today: DEMONS CAN DO DAMAGE

Our Scripture
And they come to Jesus, and see him that was possessed with the devil, and had the legion, sitting, and clothed, and in his right mind: and they were afraid (St. Mark 5:15, KJV).

Our Simple Lesson
As believers in Jesus Christ, you are faced with real enemies. You have an internal enemy. It's called the flesh. It lies to you; it deceives you. We have an external enemy. It's called the world. It seems attractive until you begin realizing everything in the world goes contrary to God's Word. And you have an infernal enemy. He is called the Devil and Satan. Demonic structures are very real for the believer. They cause spiritual blindness. They often cause radical disobedience and doubt; if you allow them to, they will derail and defeat you. They attach themselves to people, families, fathers and their sons. They attack mothers, daughters, brothers, sisters and even churches. Demons are not to be played with. In our story for the week, in St. Mark 5, you find a man who defines himself as Legion, whose demons are doing significant damage. The word "Legion" means thousands of demons. In short, Legion, is a walking fortress of demonic activity. The man lives in a graveyard and appears to be deranged and out of control. The study aim for this week is to analyze how demons do damage and stay focused on the fact that God is able to deliver His own by way of His power.

Our Serious Need To Change
A true tell tale sign that demons are attacking you is when you are bound to certain sins that will not let you go free. Every time you seek to move forward they pull you backwards. When you decide to make a significant change in your life and something surfaces that prohibits the change leaving your life in a place of darkness and bondage. It is then and only then that an ever present all powerful Lord coupled with a spirit of repentance from you heart can bring about true redemptive change. With this in mind, be careful because you could be under demonic attack and not really know it.

Our Sincere Petition
Heavenly Father, in the name of Jesus, cause spirits of darkness and demonic figures of evil to be dismissed from my life. I desire to follow You in faith and to be completely obedient to Your will, Your Word, and Your way. In The Name of Jesus, Amen.

WEEK 8: He Changed My Life Forever
Day 2

God's Word For You Today: HE'S VICIOUS TO SOME BUT HE'S A VESSEL TO THE LORD

Our Scripture
And they come to Jesus, and see him that was possessed with the devil, and had the legion, sitting, and clothed, and in his right mind: and they were afraid (St. Mark 5:15, KJV).

Our Simple Lesson
During your study this week, you are examining St. Mark 5, the very first narrative of three. In Mark 5, Jesus shows His superiority and authority over demons in verses 1-11, over disease in verses 24-35, and over death in verses 36 to the end of the text. Today, you are looking at the first narrative. And the shout of the day is what people see as vicious God sees as a vessel.

The man in the text is nameless but filled with demons. But by the time the Lord finishes working in his life, he becomes a vessel of redemptive love, with the gospel on his tongue to tell everybody what a mighty God he serves.

Our Serious Need To Change
Have you been touched by God's hand yet in a way that changes you to the point that you become a vessel of His redemptive love, a voice for the gospel to be declared through your testimony? Has your life changed since you have met the Jesus Christ? My hopeful answer is yes. If you haven't, you should ask the Lord right now to touch you like never before.

Our Sincere Petition
Spirit of the Living God, allow your presence to rest, rule, and remain in my life. Cause me, O God, to become a portrait of what repentance really looks like so that when people see me, they receive a glimpse of what your grace produces.

In The Name of Jesus, Amen.

WEEK 8: He Changed My Life Forever
Day 3

God's Word For You Today: A PICTURE IS WORTH A THOUSAND WORDS

Our Scripture
And they come to Jesus, and see him that was possessed with the devil, and had the legion, sitting, and clothed, and in his right mind: and they were afraid (St. Mark 5:15, KJV).

Our Simple Lesson
You've heard the saying before that a picture is worth a thousand words. It's true. As you look at selfies on Facebook, Instagram, Snapchat, and TikTok they all tell stories. As you look at people taking pictures all over the place with their Androids and iPhones, you must realize that these images that are being captured present to those of us who view them real life narratives that present themselves in each photograph.

If that's true, St. Mark 5:1-11, paint a wonderful picture of what redemption looks like. What does it look like for God to change a man's life who was headed to hell because he was filled with the hell he was headed to? What does it look like for God to transform us with His redemptive love, make us brand new again, deliver us from the past, bless the present, and protect the future? It looks like a demon-possessed man who's running naked in a graveyard, who sees the Lord, falls at his feet, worships, and has the demons in his life dismissed.

Our Serious Need To Change
What demons do you struggle with that are private and personal? What demonic figures have found a home in your life that cause you not to be all that God has called you to be? Here is a personal petition for you to tender today at the throne of God when you pray: God dismiss those demons in me, just like you did for the man in St. Mark 5. The great news is this, if Jesus did it before, He can and will do it again!

Our Sincere Petition
So, Lord, today I ask You humbly to look inwardly at my life and dismiss anything that is not like You. If it doesn't please You in my life, I no longer want it.

In The Name of Jesus, Amen.

WEEK 8: He Changed My Life Forever
Day 4

God's Word For You Today: A DECISION THAT CHANGES YOUR CONDITION

Our Scripture
And they come to Jesus, and see him that was possessed with the devil, and had the legion, sitting, and clothed, and in his right mind: and they were afraid (Mark 5:15, KJV).

Our Simple Lesson
One decision can change your life forever. In fact, a bad decision can put you in trouble that can mar your past and ruin your future. One mediocre decision could lead you to a place where you are stuck, stagnant, stale, and don't want to go forward. But one great decision, though it may not be popular, could change your life for the greater.

This man, in your study passage this week, makes a decision not to run from the Lord, but to run to Him. The most interesting thing about it is that before the cross, Jesus comes through a storm to meet a man coming out of a tomb. And after the cross, Jesus comes out of a tomb to meet men who are coming through a storm. Either way, we must meet Jesus and make a decision to live for Him. Repentance at its core, is the root, and fruit of what salvation looks like. It is deliverance and victory at its best.

Our Serious Need To Change
There comes a point in your walk with the Lord when you make some decisions to ask God to rid you of some habits, get rid of some demons, and put your life on another path whose trajectory is so holy that when people meet you, they meet a reasonable facsimile of Him.

Our Sincere Petition
Bless the Lord, O my soul, and all that's within me. Bless His holy name. Today, O God, I ask You to please help me with my decision-making all day long. I begin my morning with a heart of repentance that says, "I'm sorry for anything that I've done that was not pleasing to You." However, Lord, my day will be filled with decisions. Let my mind be influenced by Your Spirit all day long.

In The Name of Jesus, Amen.

WEEK 8: He Changed My Life Forever
Day 5

God's Word For You Today: YOU DO YOUR PART AND HE'LL DO HIS

Our Scripture
And they come to Jesus, and see him that was possessed with the devil, and had the legion, sitting, and clothed, and in his right mind: and they were afraid (Mark 5:15, KJV).

Our Simple Lesson
I don't know much about the law, but I understand "quid pro quo." It is Latin, and it means "this for that." You see, whenever there is a "quid pro quo" in the law, if you do this, then the law and the system does that. But in order to get that, you must first do this. We have been saying it a long time from a spiritual perspective, and it goes like this: you do your part, and God will do His. Repentance begins with a heart that says, "God, I'm sorry, and I'm changing my mind." It concludes with God doing His part, opening doors no man can close, closing doors no man can open, forgiving sins that no one can wash away, and placing your life on the solid foundation of hope that is built in Him. It is what takes place in St. Mark 5. This story should make your heart rejoice because this nameless demon-possessed man decides to do one thing: run to Jesus. His decision has a blessed idea and reality that concludes with him being seated, free, and clothed in his right mind.

Our Serious Need To Change
Whenever you decide to allow Christ to set you free you will be free indeed. When you discover that the one in bondage is you and you desire to be spiritually liberated by the power of God then and only then will real change come. When you conclude that what you need is not religion but repentance that produces real change in your life, you will see a move of God that shifts you from abysmal darkness into His marvelous light. Repentance is your part and deliverance belongs to the Lord.

Our Sincere Petition
O God, my Father, I've come to You today asking You to do for me what I cannot do for myself. If I have any hangups that keep me hung up please help me. If I have any problems that keep me from being all You've designed me to be have mercy. If I have any situations or circumstances that are causing me not to walk with You, then, God, I pray in the name of Jesus, remove it.

In The Name of Jesus, Amen.

WEEK 8: He Changed My Life Forever

Day 6

God's Word For You Today: CLOTHED IN YOUR RIGHT MIND

Our Scripture
And they come to Jesus, and see him that was possessed with the devil, and had the legion, sitting, and clothed, and in his right mind: and they were afraid (Mark 5:15, KJV).

Our Simple Lesson
The NAACP, the National Association for the Advancement of Colored People, has often carried a mantra for its organization that is very profound. It simply says, "A mind is a terrible thing to waste." Not only is the mantra profound, it is true. The Bible says, "As a man thinketh in his heart, so is he." No one can shift your mind about you like you can. No one can look at your future like you can.

The great news about repentance, as found in the portrait of this passage, is this: a demon-possessed, crazy man, living naked in a graveyard, makes a decision for Jesus. He changes his mind about where he is, which is his location, shifts his mind about his future, which is his destination, and says to God, "If you're still healing, offer me liberation." The shout of the day is the Lord hears his cry, pities his every groan, and does for him what he cannot do for himself.

Our Serious Need To Change
Do you know what God has done for others, He can do for you? The good news about the God we serve is that He is the only God whose redundancy looks redemptive. He's done it over and over again. He did it for Joshua at Jericho. He did it for Gideon at Midian. He did it for David against Goliath. In the fiery furnace, He did it in Babylon for Shadrach, Meshach, and Abednego. He can do it for you if He's done it for them.

Our Sincere Petition
And so, God, I've come today being as transparent as I can, thanking You for a spirit that lets me know You can leave me clothed and seated in my right mind. Lord, if there are any attacks against my mind right now, I pray in the name of Jesus that You cancel those assaults. Let this mind be in me, which was also in Christ. Jesus, that is my petition and prayer. It is my plea and asking.

In The Name of Jesus, Amen.

WEEK 8: He Changed My Life Forever
Day 7

God's Word For You Today: WHAT A WONDERFUL CHANGE

Our Scripture
And they come to Jesus, and see him that was possessed with the devil, and had the legion, sitting, and clothed, and in his right mind: and they were afraid (Mark 5:15, KJV).

Our Simple Lesson
I love Pastoring the Antioch Church in Beaumont, Texas, for many reasons. The people are so kind. The city is so wonderful. The closeness of our seven exits makes me feel like I live in Mayberry. You know, the town where Opie and Andy Griffith used to live. Here's the truth: Beaumont can be a blessed place, but what I really love about Beaumont is the people in whose lives I can clearly see repentance, redemption, and change. Several of my Deacons are ex-drug addicts. I love that because their testimonies are so powerful, showing how they once lived before the Lord and now how they live after meeting Him. Here is what they all ascribe to be true. "O, what a wonderful change has come over my life."

Such is the case with the man in Mark 5. His story is a similitude of those testimonies I hear from Deacons who have been delivered from crack, heroin, alcohol, and all sorts of chemicals. "O, what a wonderful change has come over my life."

Our Serious Need To Change
The wonderful change that God affords them is what He affords any and all of us who make a decision to follow Him. It happens with one decision, one about-face, one change in your direction, and one shift in your attitude and actions. Repentance is so powerful it takes a sinner out of darkness and places him in the marvelous light. The question is this today: have you made your decision yet? Please hear this, there is nobody like Him. There is nobody like Jesus who is the Christ.

Our Sincere Petition
Lord God, thank You for making a difference in my life today. I can honestly say, "O, what a wonderful change has come over me." My life is no longer the same because of You. I love You, praise You, honor You, and thank You.

In The Name of Jesus, Amen.

WEEK 8: He Changed My Life Forever
Week 8 Conclusion

HIGHER THAN THE TOP
HT3

<u>Life Application</u>
Every church in the known world, should march to the beat of three core values that should never shift or change. They are the reason the church exists. They are the raison d'être for the Church of God on the Earth. Core value number one, The Great Commission, "Go ye therefore, teach and baptize." That's what the scripture says the people of God should do. Core value number two, The Great Commandment, "Go with love." That's the new commandment Jesus gives to us. Core value number three, "The Great Calling." We are to be fishing for the souls of lost people the world-over.

These core values are the reason any and every church on the planet is present. But when you look at your work in the body of Christ, do you see these core values being lived out everyday? Do you ever share Christ with anyone? When do you share the love of God in servitude and action? Do you ever intentionally seek to win people that are lost to Jesus? Be honest with your answers.

Here is what I want to offer you as a suggestion from one believer to another get busy doing what we are called to do. Your church has ministry constructs that offer you the ability to perform these core values without trying hard. Just become a part, and as you become a part, you'll fulfill The Great Commission, The Great Commandment, and The Great Calling. It is going to be life-changing for you and a blessing for those with whom you share Jesus Christ with.

WEEK 9: Three Strikes and You're In

Day 1

God's Word For You Today: HE MISSED IT THREE TIMES

Our Scripture
And entering into the sepulchre, they saw a young man sitting on the right side, clothed in a long white garment; and they were affrighted. And he saith unto them, Be not affrighted: Ye seek Jesus of Nazareth, which was crucified: he is risen; he is not here: behold the place where they laid him. But go your way, tell his disciples and Peter that "He goeth before you into Galilee: there shall ye see him, as he said unto you (St. Mark 16:5-7, KJV).

Our Simple Lesson
I used to love playing baseball in my neighborhood, Lakewood. My neighborhood in Northeast Houston was filled with magnificent people who, in my past, were trapped in poverty. Baseball was my game. We didn't have a diamond to play on and the home plate was a crushed beer can in the street. The second base was a Ford Ltd on four flats. The first base was a tree in my neighbor's yard. The third base was a tree in my other neighbor's yard. And well, a home run meant that you hit the ball far enough to run and touch all three bases and make it home. We were in the World Series of the Ghetto. The young boys from Lakewood were playing the boys from Pinewood. Our worst batter was up to bat with a runner on second base. His name was Timothy Norman, but we called him Tim Tim for short. The first pitch came; he swung and missed. The second pitch came; he swung and missed. The third pitch came, and he swung and missed. It reminds me of Peter as we examine our scripture for the week. Peter denies the Lord three times. The great news is he missed it all three times, but the Lord never fired him. He never called him out. It was as if to say, Hey, Peter, you've had three strikes, and you're still in.

Our Serious Need To Change
Peter knows he's missed it. He is not looking at anyone else's life but his. Can I ask you a question? In what ways have you missed it lately? What is causing you to miss it? For you to repent means, "God, I don't plan on missing it again."

Our Sincere Petition
Lord as I take a close look at my life today, I can see spaces and places where I've missed it. May I ask You, God, please don't throw me away, don't give up on me, don't delete me. Just give me another chance, and I promise to do my best. In The Name of Jesus, Amen.

WEEK 9: Three Strikes and You're In

Day 2

God's Word For You Today: THANK GOD HE DIDN'T GIVE UP ON YOU

Our Scripture
And entering into the sepulchre, they saw a young man sitting on the right side, clothed in a long white garment; and they were affrighted. And he saith unto them, Be not affrighted: Ye seek Jesus of Nazareth, which was crucified: he is risen; he is not here: behold the place where they laid him. But go your way, tell his disciples and Peter that he goeth before you into Galilee: there shall ye see him, as he said unto you (St. Mark 16:5-7, KJV).

Our Simple Lesson
In your passage for the week, it's Resurrection Sunday morning. An angel has made a magnificent announcement that the one they seek is risen. He is not there. He is alive! What a wonderful day it was for all of Christianity for an angel to announce that the one who was crucified, dead, and buried had been resurrected. Yet, my friend, as you study this passage, it is important to realize that the angel announces to the women that they should tell the disciples to meet Jesus in the city. But the most incredible part of the lesson comes when he includes Peter too. You see, Peter had just denied Him three times. He had just turned his back on the Lord, knowing that he would deny Him because Jesus told him he would do so. You know, it's one thing to get hit by a bus. It's another thing to get hit by a bus that you know is coming. Peter knew it was coming and still missed it, not once, twice, but thrice. Just like the Lord did not give up on Peter, He has never given up on you.

Our Serious Need To Change
Peter needs to make a change, and he knows it. There are changes you need to make, and you also know it. To repent means to change. What does repentance really look like? It looks like the person who stared you in the face this morning while you were brushing your teeth that knows what mercy feels like. It looks like the person who has missed more than three times, but God did not fire you, but kept you on the team. With this in mind, you owe God more than you will ever be able to repay Him.

Our Sincere Petition
Thank You, Jesus, for the decisions I have made in my life for the better that have been prompted and pushed by the Spirit of the living God. Thank God for holding my hand, letting me stand, and empowering me to march on. In The Name of Jesus, Amen.

WEEK 9: Three Strikes and You're In
Day 3

God's Word For You Today: TO KNOW BETTER IS ONE THING TO DO BETTER IS ANOTHER

Our Scripture

And entering into the sepulchre, they saw a young man sitting on the right side, clothed in a long white garment; and they were affrighted. And he saith unto them, Be not affrighted: Ye seek Jesus of Nazareth, which was crucified: he is risen; he is not here: behold the place where they laid him. But go your way, tell his disciples and Peter that he goeth before you into Galilee: there shall ye see him, as he said unto you (St. Mark 16:5-7, KJV).

Our Simple Lesson

My mother was a disciplinarian. She said things once, and after that, she would begin laying hands without oil. It was discipline at its finest. However, she didn't exploit her discipline as if to hurt her children. It was designed to train her children. There were times when my mother knew that we didn't know any better, and she would spare us with her mercy and grant us her grace. God is similar to this in that there are times He knows that to know better is one thing, but to do better is another. Now, ignorance of sin does not make the sin any less. It just makes mercy that much greater. Peter knows better, but he doesn't do better. He knows that he's going to deny the Lord, but he still denies Him. The benefit and blessing of the story is that instead of finding judgment and wrath, Peter finds grace and mercy.

Our Serious Need To Change

The great news for your life today is that God is meeting you in this message, in this book right now with a grace you will never fully understand and a mercy that's made new every morning. It is not that you're waiting on God to do something new with you. God is waiting for you to do something great with Him. His hand is open. His heart is ready. His Cross is vacant. His tomb is empty. His spirit is real, and His Word is true. Make your decision for Jesus and march on.

Our Sincere Petition

Thank You, Lord Jesus Christ, for helping me do better. Because knowing better is one thing, but doing better is another. God, in areas and times where I fail, falter, or fall short, grant me the grace and mercy You gave Peter because my heart loves You with everything in it.

In The Name of Jesus, Amen.

WEEK 9: Three Strikes and You're In

Day 4

God's Word For You Today: O TO BE KEPT BY JESUS

Our Scripture
And entering into the sepulchre, they saw a young man sitting on the right side, clothed in a long white garment; and they were affrighted. And he saith unto them, Be not affrighted: Ye seek Jesus of Nazareth, which was crucified: he is risen; he is not here: behold the place where they laid him. But go your way, tell his disciples and Peter that he goeth before you into Galilee: there shall ye see him, as he said unto you (St. Mark 16:5-7, KJV).

Our Simple Lesson
To be kept by the Lord is to be kept for sure. When Peter denied the Lord, it was on the day that they marched Him from judgment hall to judgment hall. Three days after the resurrection, Peter was invited to join the disciples in Jerusalem for a significant meeting with the Messiah, Jesus Christ. Here is a question that should make you really ponder and think: Who kept Peter after he made the mistake and before the resurrection? Here's the answer: The same God who kept Peter before he ever knew the Lord and the same God who would keep him until the day he died. See, here is the truth: the Lord has kept you your whole life. Even when you were completely unaware of it, the hand of a merciful, kind, sovereign God has been holding you together. It's why repentance makes so much sense. Why not change your mind for Him because He has already made up his mind about you?

Our Serious Need To Change
God awaits moments of opportunity when you run out of options, cannot help yourself, and need Him to help you because He is our only option. God loves being the only option because He wants you to know that all opportunity comes from Him. Today, you have a chance to make some positive changes in your life, repent, change in some ways, shift some thoughts, and get rid of some habits. And God says, when you decide to do it, you will discover I've been keeping you the whole time.

Our Sincere Petition
Lord, thank You for keeping me when I was not trying to live right. Thank you for holding me when I was in a den of demons and thought I was having a good time. O praise your name, O Lord, for being so gracious and merciful to me.

In The Name of Jesus, Amen.

WEEK 9: Three Strikes and You're In
Day 5

God's Word For You Today: GOD SAYS, CHANGE YOUR MIND ABOUT ME

Our Scripture

And entering into the sepulchre, they saw a young man sitting on the right side, clothed in a long white garment; and they were affrighted. And he saith unto them, Be not affrighted: Ye seek Jesus of Nazareth, which was crucified: he is risen; he is not here: behold the place where they laid him. But go your way, tell his disciples and Peter that he goeth before you into Galilee: there shall ye see him, as he said unto you (St. Mark 16:5-7, KJV).

Our Simple Lesson

Not long ago, I was approached by one of my faithful parishioners who posed an interesting existential interrogative towards me. She simply asked one evening after Thursday night Bible study, "Pastor, what does God really want from me?" I paused and contemplated, and as I thought, the Spirit of the Lord impressed these words upon me. "God wants you to change your mind about Him." God is shouting from Heaven. "Change your mind about Me." It's the root of what repentance actually is and what it looks like. "Change your mind about My provisions. I am going to take care of you. Change your mind about my protection. I'm going to wrap my loving arms around you. Change your mind about My person. There is no one on Earth like Me," says the Lord. "Change your mind about My peace. I have torn down the middle wall that separates us. You now have access to me. Change your mind about my purpose for your life on Earth; I have use for you. You're My friend, and I want to use your life for My glory.

Our Serious Need To Change

It is one thing for you to have a vision for your life, but it is another for God to have one. When you change your mind about the Lord, you will ultimately see a change in your future because God will use His Spirit to fill your body, guide your thoughts, and redirect your destiny.

Our Sincere Petition

Lord, everybody seems to have a plan for my life. My teacher had a plan. My coach had a plan. My boss had a plan. My parents had plans. Lord, I even realized the devil had plans. But today, I want Your plan for my life, so I'm changing my mind about You, and I say to You at this very moment: You order my steps, You guide my fate, and You take control of my future.

In The Name of Jesus, Amen.

WEEK 9: Three Strikes and You're In

Day 6

God's Word For You Today: REPENTANCE AND FORGIVENESS GO TOGETHER

Our Scripture

And entering into the sepulchre, they saw a young man sitting on the right side, clothed in a long white garment; and they were affrighted. And he saith unto them, Be not affrighted: Ye seek Jesus of Nazareth, which was crucified: he is risen; he is not here: behold the place where they laid him. But go your way, tell his disciples and Peter that he goeth before you into Galilee: there shall ye see him, as he said unto you (St. Mark 16:5-7, KJV).

Our Simple Lesson

There are some things in life that just go well together: cereal and milk, greens and yams, rice and gravy. It's just designed to go together. Cake and ice cream, you name it, were some things that went together. They just fit well. Repentance and forgiveness are such for the Christian. In your study passage this week, you find a repentant Peter weeping and sorrowful for his sins in Mark 14: 34-46. But when you begin to look carefully at Mark 16, the repentance of 14 leads to forgiveness in 16. If Peter hadn't lamented, wept, and felt sorry for his mistake, the chapter that you are celebrating today in this week would have read differently. I do not believe the angel would have been instructed to bring Peter. But because he was weeping and saddened by his actions, the Lord said, I can use a man like that on my team. Repentance and forgiveness go together. They work together on your behalf.

Our Serious Need To Change

One of the most dangerous things in the life of any Christian is unrepentant sin. One thing you should do regularly as a believer in the Lord is repent of sinful actions and activities that were not pleasing to God. To go with unrepentant sin leads you to a place of divine discipline. The Bible says that God has no sons or children that He does not discipline. Discipline finds the unrepentant believer who says, "I'm not saying I'm sorry, and if I did say it, I didn't mean it." I encourage you to take a moment out of every day and tell the Lord, "Lord, whatever I've done that's not pleasing in your sight, please forgive me."

Our Sincere Petition

God, I have prayed for many things in my life. I prayed for the healing of loved ones, the salvation of friends, and for blessings that will only come from You to us on Earth. But today, I pray neither of those petitions. I pray that You be merciful to me and accept my sincerest apology for any sins I've committed. In The Name of Jesus, Amen.

WEEK 9: Three Strikes and You're In

Day 7

God's Word For You Today: GOOD NEWS YOU'RE STILL ON THE TEAM

Our Scripture

And entering into the sepulchre, they saw a young man sitting on the right side, clothed in a long white garment; and they were affrighted. And he saith unto them, Be not affrighted: Ye seek Jesus of Nazareth, which was crucified: he is risen; he is not here: behold the place where they laid him. But go your way, tell his disciples and Peter that he goeth before you into Galilee: there shall ye see him, as he said unto you (Mark 16:5-7, KJV).

Our Simple Lesson

You began this week's study with a narrative of a friend named Tim Tim, who was at bat for the Ghetto World Series of the Hood. Lakewood was playing Pinewood. If you didn't read that story, go back and read week 9, day 1. Here's the shout of the lesson: Tim Tim never gets a hit. He strikes out not only once. He strikes out enough to strike out three times. In baseball, you get three strikes, and you're out. Tim Tim may have had nine cuts at it. He never even gets a foul tip. But the shout of the day is Tim Tim's father, Mr. Norman, had another son that he made bat for him. You see, Tim Tim never did get a hit. He missed it every time, so his older brother John came to bat for him. John told Tim Tim to stand over to his right. He then told the young man pitching for Pinewood, "throw the ball." And when that ball came near that plate, John Rodney Norman hit it so far it faded into the setting of the sun. TimTim took off running with a joy in his step and a leap in his stride. And to the best of my recollection, I can remember him saying he did it just for me! He hit it just for me! He did it just for me! He touched all the bases, and we won the game. Tim Tim could never get it together, but his elder brother hit it for him. This is what makes Peter's testimony so crucial in this concluding gospel verse that we are reading. As the gospel of Mark presents this moment after the resurrection of Jesus, the celebration is that Peter never gets it all right. However, he has an older brother, who is Jesus Christ, who bats for him, who, on Calvary, knocked it out of the park. Peter had to pick up grace, hold on to mercy, run, and touch every base.

Our Serious Need To Change

Not only is this what Peter had to do, but it is God's commission to the repentant and forgiven believer. Don't worry about hitting it all the time. Your job is to run, touch every base, and tell everybody who did it for you!

WEEK 9: Three Strikes and You're In

Our Sincere Petition
Thank You, Jesus, for being an elder brother who hits for me when I strike out and for letting me remain on Your team.

In The Name of Jesus, Amen.

Week 9 Conclusion

HIGHER THAN THE TOP
HT3

Life Application
If you are like most, you struck out a long time ago. Truth be told, you've had so many misses you can no longer count them. They are innumerable, yet God has counted every one of them. What makes repentance so powerful is you change your mind about the God who's never changed His mind about you. When you finally come to grips with the love of God, the grace of God, the peace of God, the purpose of God, and the plan of God it should bring tears to your eyes. When you finally realize that He's never changed His mind about you, it makes you want to live for Him in a whole new way, with a whole new passion. The local church is a valuable part of the life of a believer on Earth. Your church has a vision to fulfill. It exalts the Savior, evangelizes the sinner, equips the save, edifies the saint, and encourages every soul. With in mind, take your faith in God to the next level by praying more often, studying God's Word more intently and sharing your love for Jesus Christ with others.

WEEK 10: I'll Never Be the Same Again

Day 1

God's Word For You Today: SOME CHANGE REQUIRES CONFRONTATION

Our Scripture
And as he journeyed, he came near Damascus: and suddenly there shined round about him a light from Heaven: and he fell to the earth, and heard a voice saying unto him, Saul, Saul, why persecutest thou me (Acts 9:3-4, KJV)?

Our Simple Lesson
There are times when change comes easily. You change a pillowcase or a sheet on a bed. You change socks and the color of your accessories without much thought. It's a change. But real, radical change is often confrontational. The person who eats a poor diet filled with saturated fat doesn't stop eating fried chicken, oxtail, and pork bones until they realize that they have arteries that are clogged. The person who sips every day and continues doing such doesn't really stop drinking until they know they have sclerosis of the liver. Radical change requires confrontation. That is what happens on the Damascus Road in Acts 9. The Apostle Paul is knocked to the ground and blinded temporarily by a light that shines from Heaven. He hears a voice that says, "Saul, Saul, why persecuted thou Me?" It is radical, yet it produces the greatest preacher and Apostle of the Lord given to us in the Greek New Testament. The writer of over two-thirds of its books comes from this one man, the Apostle Paul.

Our Serious Need To Change
What has happened in your life that produced radical change? Was it a death in the family, a bad automobile accident, or the termination of a job? What took place in your life that made you say, "I need God, and I won't continue on the path that I'm going."

Our Sincere Petition
Lord, this today, I thank You for the radical changes You have produced in my life. Without them, I would not be where I am. I trust You, I love You, I need You. Thank You for continuing to change me into the image of Your son.

In The Name of Jesus, Amen.

WEEK 10: I'll Never Be the Same Again
Day 2

God's Word For You Today: LORD, WHAT DO YOU WANT ME TO DO

Our Scripture
And as he journeyed, he came near Damascus: and suddenly there shined round about him a light from Heaven: and he fell to the earth, and heard a voice saying unto him, Saul, Saul, why persecutest thou me (Acts 9:3-4, KJV)?

Our Simple Lesson
Your study passage for the week is Acts 9. Please take a moment to read it because the story is simply amazing. Paul is on the Damascus Road. He is a persecutor of Christians. He actually hates the church. A bright light from Heaven shines upon him. He fell to the ground, and was blinded. And to make matters even more interesting, he hears the voice of the Lord say, "Saul, Saul, Why persecuted thou Me?" Please take a moment and read all of Acts 9. It will only take a moment.

Here is what you're going to discover: when Paul finally is broken so that he can be blessed and when he is bruised enough for God to use, he asks the Lord a question that serves as the core and center of his repentance. The question is, "Lord, what do You want me to do?"

Our Serious Need To Change
Here is a great devotional question to begin this lesson with: has God broken you to the point that you cried out, "God, what do You want me to do?" Life doesn't improve until you're bruised like Paul is in the passage, until you say, "God, whatever You want me to do, I'll do it." Moments like this produce redemptive repentance that is life-changing.

Our Sincere Petition
Eternal God, my Father, I do not have to hear a loud voice from Heaven or have a spotlight shine upon me before I reach a place where I simply say, "What do You want me to do?" I love you enough to ask in prayer, "Lord, what do You want from me right now?" I will do it by faith, and with joy. I will achieve it, if it makes You happy and if you are happy, I promise be satisfied.

In The Name of Jesus, Amen.

WEEK 10: I'll Never Be the Same Again
Day 3

God's Word For You Today: EYES WITH NO VISION

Our Scripture
And as he journeyed, he came near Damascus: and suddenly there shined round about him a light from Heaven: and he fell to the earth, and heard a voice saying unto him, Saul, Saul, why persecutest thou me (Acts 9:3-4, KJV)?

Our Simple Lesson
Helen Keller is one of the most wonderful life testimonies of endurance, perseverance, and overcoming. Once, she made a remark that I felt was both profound and prolific. Keller said, "The only thing worse than being blind is having eyes with no vision."

The Apostle Paul understood this statement years before she ever declared it. While he is on the Damascus Road, he's blinded for a season. Interestingly, he does not see clearly until he can't see physically. Sometimes, in the process of complete repentance, God has to bruise you to bless you, to allow life to hurt you just to help you, to permit the worst of times to produce the sweetest outcomes ever.

Our Serious Need To Change
There are times in your life when God will permit and allow suffering, but there are moments when God designs that suffering to produce different things. Sometimes, it is to get you to go in another direction, to make you put your blinker on, make a U-turn, and go completely in the opposite direction in life. This is a moment of true repentance. It brings you to the place of a change that says it took God to make this happen.

Our Sincere Petition
Spirit of the Living God, rest upon me today so that what comes from me is a change that pleasing to You. And, God, allow me to see You in the spirit and receive You for who You are, Lord, Christ, God, and Redeemer. Thank You, Jesus, for saving me, and thank You, O God, for making a difference in my life.

In The Name of Jesus, Amen.

WEEK 10: I'll Never Be the Same Again
Day 4

God's Word For You Today: RESTORATION: GOD ALWAYS HAS A PLAN

Our Scripture
And as he journeyed, he came near Damascus: and suddenly there shined round about him a light from Heaven: and he fell to the earth, and heard a voice saying unto him, Saul, Saul, why persecutest thou me (Acts 9:3-4, KJV)?

Our Simple Lesson
Not long ago, I did an academic interview for a student working on a PhD in preaching. I was simply asked, "What's my philosophy of preaching?" What are my theological perspectives when it regards declaring the good news of Jesus Christ in the Bible? My answer was very simple. I am a theocentric redemptionist. I believe that God is always in the process of restoring that which belongs to Him. In short, God always has a plan. In your passage this week, God's plan was to use Paul as a mighty warrior, a servant who would preach, proclaim, and declare the gospel with such passion that the Earth would have never seen another man who would do as great a work as Paul. It took God to break him, bless him, restore him, and renew him for the redeemed purpose planned for his life. Paul would live out God's plan in such a way until he would make the statement, "I am now ready to be offered." The Apostle Paul ran his race, finished his course, and kept his faith, but it was because God had a plan for his life the entire time.

Our Serious Need To Change
Have you come to grips with the reality that God really has a plan for you? You know it is God's plan when it has nothing to do with the plans you have for yourself. God's plan is so profound that it makes you uncomfortable. It is that moment when you say, "Not me. I cannot do that. This is not why I'm here." And God says, "You were made for the assignment"

Our Sincere Petition
Lord, I want to know my purpose. I desire to discover it. If You would be so kind, O Lord, reveal what You wish for me. It will lead me to a degree of repentance that is needed and necessary for my journey. Thank You for the revelation. I will receive it by faith. In The Name of Jesus, Amen.

WEEK 10: I'll Never Be the Same Again

Day 5

God's Word For You Today: A STREET CALLED STRAIGHT

Our Scripture
And as he journeyed, he came near Damascus: and suddenly there shined round about him a light from Heaven: and he fell to the earth, and heard a voice saying unto him, Saul, Saul, why persecutest thou me (Acts 9:3-4, KJV)?

Our Simple Lesson
When Paul was been blinded, he remained in that condition for three days. He goes on a fast because his life has changed. He understands that God is up to something. He then is led by the Lord and taken to a city. Interestingly, while Paul is in deep prayer and contemplation, the Lord summons a servant named Ananias. God tells Ananias, "There is a man that I plan to use. You will find him in this city on Street called Straight. His name is Saul." Isn't it amazing that God always has a servant willing to do His work and who is ready to aid you, but you don't even know they exist? And isn't it overwhelmingly ironic that Paul, who had been living crooked, ends up on a street called Straight? That is what happens when repentance takes place. God moves you to Straight Street.

Our Serious Need To Change
Here's the real truth of the matter: some of the streets in your life has been made straight by the grace of God, while others need some attention. There are two ways to get to Straight Street. Either you can make the U-turns necessary to get you there, or God will offer you some assistance. Trust me, when I offer you this wisdom, it is easier if you make the changes up front.

Our Sincere Petition
I need Thee, O God, in gracious, merciful ways. Right now, as I pray to You, You know, like I do, that every street in my life is not straight, so please help me. There are areas where there are pot holes, speed bumps, places where I should not travel at all. Be merciful to me. Be gracious towards me. Take my hand and lead me gently to the place that will bring You ultimate glory.

In The Name of Jesus, Amen.

WEEK 10: I'll Never Be the Same Again
Day 6

God's Word For You Today: GOOD NEWS, U-TURNS ALLOWED

Our Scripture
And as he journeyed, he came near Damascus: and suddenly there shined round about him a light from Heaven: and he fell to the earth, and heard a voice saying unto him, Saul, Saul, why persecutest thou me (Acts 9:3-4, KJV)?

Our Simple Lesson
Not long ago, while in a city for revival, I was being chauffeured by a very kind gentleman from the church. He was a servant, a deacon, and a lead assistant to the pastor. He was wonderful as a person, but as a driver, he struggled a bit. When we got ready to get to the hotel, he missed his exit. We were trying to find places for him to turn around. I was tired and ready for bed; no sign read U-turns allowed. We journeyed for 10 minutes in the wrong direction, going at a high speed. Finally, he saw a sign that said, "U-turns allowed." He put his blinker on with great passion and expediency, made a zipping U-turn, and started traveling toward the right destination. In our passage, the Apostle Paul fully understands what it is like to travel in the wrong direction and then suddenly make a U-turn. But the good news is that sometimes you need a sign that can assist you. God sends signs that it's time to make a U-turn. Don't miss yours.

Our Serious Need To Change
When it comes to making U-turns, God places signs all around you. They are warning signs of His grace and mercy, placed there in kindness and compassion. You've just been trained to ignore them, to walk past them. But to heed them is to bless yourself. If you desire to bless yourself, heed the warning signs. Make the needed and necessary adjustments and changes, and celebrate the U-turn He has made in you.

Our Sincere Petition
Thank You, Jesus, for moments when U-turns are permitted without getting a ticket. Hallelujah to Your name for the changes You've already made and for the magnificent, redemptive changes that are yet to come.

In The Name of Jesus, Amen.

WEEK 10: I'll Never Be the Same Again

Day 7

God's Word For You Today: RELIGION IS ONE THING, BUT REPENTANCE IS SOMETHING ELSE

Our Scripture
And as he journeyed, he came near Damascus: and suddenly there shined round about him a light from Heaven: and he fell to the earth, and heard a voice saying unto him, Saul, Saul, why persecutest thou me (Acts 9:3-4, KJV)?

Our Simple Lesson
If there is only one thing I want you to carry from this week's study session and passage, it is this: religion is one thing, but repentance is something else. Paul was a very religious man. He was a Pharisee regarding the law. That meant he knew the Bible's first five books by memory. He could literally quote Genesis, Exodus, Leviticus, Numbers, and Deuteronomy without a note in front of him. He knew the law. He was an expert in keeping the outward signs of a religious man. Just because you are religious does not mean that you have a good relationship with God. Relationships with God begin with a mindset and a heart of repentance. Do not ever forget this.

Our Serious Need To Change
Religion is a good thing, but it's hard work. A relationship that begins with repentance is easy work and does not need religion. God is not looking for prisoners. He wants friends. God is not looking for someone who will love Him partially. He wants someone who will love Him totally. And that love begins with a heart that says, Lord, repentance is exactly what I need. Repent means to change your mind, to feel sorry about your sin, to change your king and your kingdom, and to make the adjustments necessary to bring a smile to the face of your master. That is what repentance is all about.

Our Sincere Petition
O God, my God, how excellent is Your name and all the earth. When I pause to pray, I cannot help but be thankful that I was raised in a space where Your name was proclaimed. And, Father, I thank You, even now, that I have moved past religion to a relationship because I know what repentance is all about.

In The Name of Jesus, Amen.

WEEK 10: I'll Never Be the Same Again
Week 10 Conclusion

HIGHER THAN THE TOP
HT3

Life Application

There are moments when I observe people serving at the church where I am privileged to Pastor, and I often ask what their testimonies are. It is how I get to know some of our members. I will pause and ask a greeter to tell me his or her story. I'll personally pick a Deacon because of his testimony. Sometimes, I look at choir members and ask them, "So, tell me what the Lord has done for you." And you know what I found in common? Wounded people work better. The people who have not been through the most are the greatest servants of all. The people who have seen life's tough times are the servants who persevere and give God their best. Isn't it most interesting that God uses those He has bruised to serve Him in the greatest capacity?

I'll never forget when God literally changed my life forever. A drunk driver hit me head-on. Isn't it amazing? I had to be hit by a drunk driver. However, that accident produced the preacher you see and hear today. As you look at this moment of life application and take faith higher than the top, in what ways has God bruised you? In what capacity could you do more for God? You have a church with a vision. You have a church with core values. With this in mind, here is a challenge I have for you, find a way for the hurt of your past to bless someone who can grow from your experiences today. You will never live to regret it.

WEEK 11: The Answer is Knocking

Day 1

God's Word For You Today: DON'T YOU HEAR HIM KNOCKING

Our Scripture
As many as I love, I rebuke and chasten: be zealous therefore, and repent. Behold, I stand at the door, and knock: if any man hear my voice, and open the door, I will come in to him, and will sup with him, and he with me (Rev. 3:19-20, KJV).

Our Simple Lesson
I'll never forget the day I was expecting a very important package at my home. I had been tracking it, looking for it, waiting on it, but it hadn't yet arrived. I was sitting watching television, doing everything that I could possibly do to catch up with work that I was behind on, when my wonderful wife simply asked me, "Don't you hear him knocking?" I'm like, who is she talking about? What knocking could she possibly be referring to? The package I was looking for was being delivered, and the answer was knocking the entire time. As we begin our time together this week, you are in the book of Revelation. It is that magnificent book that concludes the Greek New Testament in the Bible. Oftentimes, people fear it, but you should rejoice in it as a believer because, in the end, those who love Christ, will win. Today, you are looking at the church of Laodicea, of which Jesus cautions them to be quick to repent, to change their minds, to stop going in the direction they're going in because they are lukewarm but feel like they are rich and well off. It is proof that just because you have things does not mean that you have a grip on the main thing that seeks to have a grip on you. And that is to know the true and living God for yourself.

Our Serious Need To Change
Oftentimes in life, God knocks. The good thing about Him knocking is that He's doing it in a way that He wants you to hear Him and repent. Repentance is just making the positive changes God wants you to make. With this in mind, you have made it very difficult, but the truth is, God says, "Since you belong to Me, I have a different route for you to take." And it requires some redemptive changes. Embrace them. They will always bless you.

Our Sincere Petition
Unto Thee, O God, do I place my trust. Thankfully and joyfully, I have come into Your presence, and, Lord, today, I can hear You summoning me, knocking for me, letting me know that there is more yet to come. With this at heart, O God, whatever You desire of me, I will do it. In The Name of Jesus, Amen.

WEEK 11: The Answer is Knocking
Day 2

God's Word For You Today: IT'S RUDE NOT TO ANSWER THE DOOR

Our Scripture
As many as I love, I rebuke and chasten: be zealous therefore, and repent. Behold, I stand at the door, and knock: if any man hear my voice, and open the door, I will come in to him, and will sup with him, and he with me (Rev. 3:19-20, KJV).

Our Simple Lesson
There have been times that I've heard people knocking on my door and just refuse to answer. Okay, don't judge me. I'm as human as you are. Simply put, solicitors can get on my last nerve. It's an intrusion, almost like a pop-up advertisement, while you're reading an important article on the internet. It's unwanted and unwarranted. Yet, I find myself, when someone knocks, simply opening the door. Why? Because it's rude not to answer the door when you hear someone knocking.

As you study our scripture passage for the week, one of the most beautiful pictures of Jesus in the Bible is Him knocking at the door of the Church of Laodicea. In spite of their condition of arrogance, wealth, and prosperity, they are described in the passage as poor, blind, and naked. Yet in their wretched condition, a holy, righteous, loving, caring, and compassionate God still knocks. Here is the conclusion of the matter: it's rude not to answer.

Our Serious Need To Change
In what ways has the Lord knocked, and you've ignored him? I mean, the truth is, you can hear it; you know it's there, but you've just learned how to tune Him out. I suggest to you that when the Lord knocks, it's out of love and compassion, care, and consolation for your journey on Earth that will ultimately end at His feet in eternity.

Our Sincere Petition
Lord, whenever You knock, it is my desire to answer. And, God, whatever direction You desire for my life to journey in, by faith, I will do it. Thank You for being the God who knocks even when there are times I choose not to answer.

In The Name of Jesus, Amen.

WEEK 11: The Answer is Knocking

Day 3

God's Word For You Today: HE'S KNOCKING BECAUSE HE WANTS TO GET BACK IN

Our Scripture
As many as I love, I rebuke and chasten: be zealous therefore, and repent. Behold, I stand at the door, and knock: if any man hear my voice, and open the door, I will come in to him, and will sup with him, and he with me (Rev. 3:19-20, KJV).

Our Simple Lesson
When my children were younger, I used to play games around the house with them. One of the games I would often play was my version of "hide and seek." I would hide them in their room to try to get rid of them for a moment's rest and close the door and hold the handle. Okay, don't judge me. I know it sounds cruel, but I'm their father, so I wasn't trying to hurt them, and, of course, I was going to open the door, but I just love to hear them knocking. I'll never forget one day I put my son on the outside of the door, and he just knocked and knocked and knocked. Finally, I heard his mother's voice say, "Honey, he's knocking because he wants to get back in."

Today, as you spend time with the Lord in the study of Revelation and the study of the Church of Laodicea and their need to repent remember this, God is still knowing. Your Lord keeps knocking because He wants to get back in. Here is the truth: you don't knock on a door unless you seek admittance to get into the place that the door blocks you from getting into. The Lord Jesus Christ is knocking at the heart of the door of the church, and He is saying, "I still want in."

Our Serious Need To Change
If there was ever a time the church of the living God needed a revival that would lead to repentance, it is now. The great news of the day, however, is this: our Redemptive Master is still knocking, and if He's knocking, it's because He wants to get back in.

Our Sincere Petition
Lord, my heart is open to You. My soul is ready to receive You. My spirit, O God, is thirsty for You. My hands, O God, are lifted towards You. I surrender it all to You. Jesus take up residence in every part of my life. The door of my soul is open to You.

In The Name of Jesus, Amen.

WEEK 11: The Answer is Knocking

Day 4

God's Word For You Today: WHO GAVE GOD AN EVICTION NOTICE

Our Scripture
As many as I love, I rebuke and chasten: be zealous therefore, and repent. Behold, I stand at the door, and knock: if any man hear my voice, and open the door, I will come in to him, and will sup with him, and he with me (Rev. 3:19-20, KJV).

Our Simple Lesson
As you read the narrative that is presented for you in this week's biblical study, you should find it problematic. You see, Jesus, who is the head of the church, is outside of the church, knocking, trying to get in. Doesn't that bother you? I mean, how can He be the one who would die for the church, suffer for the church, literally be persecuted in public, nailed to a tree alive for the church, be the head of the church, and now have to knock to get in it? Isn't this problematic? You have to ask yourself the question, how did He put get out? Who gave God an eviction notice? Perhaps it was in the pulpit, the lessons He wanted to teach were no longer attractive to people; and maybe, as a Deacon, perhaps the prayers He prayed were no longer helpful; or maybe even as a choir member, the songs He was singing seemed antiquated; or perhaps as an usher, He just wasn't up beat enough to stand at the door. We don't know how He got put out, but here's what we do know: no one has even noticed that He is missing. Here is the word of God for the day: if there was ever a time that you needed Jesus Christ and the cross of our Master open on display and leading us, it is right now.

Our Serious Need To Change
If you can see any part of your life where God is not present, you need to have the Lord there right now. If there is any part of your life that is absent from the presence of your Creator, it's because you have given God an eviction notice, and you don't even know it. Invite Him back into those places today. It is the picture-perfect portrait of what repentance is all about.

Our Sincere Petition
Lord, there is no place or space in my life where I do not want You to lead me. Lead me, O God, and guide me, is my sincere supplication.

In The Name of Jesus, Amen.

WEEK 11: The Answer is Knocking
Day 5

God's Word For You Today: HURRY UP AND HANDLE YOUR BUSINESS

Our Scripture
As many as I love, I rebuke and chasten: be zealous therefore, and repent. Behold, I stand at the door, and knock: if any man hear my voice, and open the door, I will come in to him, and will sup with him, and he with me (Rev. 3:19-20, KJV).

Our Simple Lesson
Deadlines really do matter, and when you find yourself pressed with a bill before they begin changing colors it is enough to make you hurry up and handle your business. When you read the book of Revelation and you get to Chapter 3, the last of the seven churches, the Church of Laodicea, is in the worst condition ever. It is the last church of the Church Age, and it is found wretched, miserable, poor, and blind. In fact, it is in such horrible condition until it is in a place that no church on Earth has ever been in before. Jesus is now outside of it. Yet the good news is the Lord cautions the church to be zealous and repent. Of course, by now, you know that the word "repent" means to feel sorry for your sins and make a change, and to turn and go in the opposite direction. But the word "zealous" here attracts me. It means to hurry. Be expedient. Do it now. The idea is for the church of the living God to hurry up and handle its business, to let God be the God of His own church. It's amazing. God could produce a hostile takeover if He wanted to, but He wants a people who want Him to lead and desire to worship Him.

Our Serious Need To Change
There are moments in your personal pilgrimage with the Potter where you know that you need to be quick to make some changes. If you can see the enemy trying to wipe you out, you need to be quick to handle your business. If you are on the verge of really giving up on the faith, or if you're in a place where doubt and dismay are overwhelming you, hurry up and handle your business. If you are involved in matters that don't please God, you don't have time to wait. Hurry and handle your business while time persists.

Our Sincere Petition
Lord, I've been in a hurry for so many things that were not even important. I found myself rushing through red lights to get to a place that had nothing to do with You. Today, O God, I am zealous toward repentance. I am going to quickly make whatever changes are needed and necessary that will bless my life and honor You. In The Name of Jesus, Amen.

WEEK 11: The Answer is Knocking
Day 6

God's Word For You Today: GET OFF THE FENCE

Our Scripture
As many as I love, I rebuke and chasten: be zealous therefore, and repent. Behold, I stand at the door, and knock: if any man hear my voice, and open the door, I will come in to him, and will sup with him, and he with me (Rev. 3:19-20, KJV).

Our Simple Lesson
When I was a kid growing up, you had to play outside. There was no such thing as playing inside. In fact, I often got into trouble for playing ball in the house. So you had to play outside. And after playing for a while, we would just sit on the fence. It was a nice place to sit. We could look at all that was going on in the neighborhood. When we were nearly in the street and just about out of the yard, our mother would often say, "Don't go out of this yard," so we would sit on the fence. That is where many of us are located today, on the fence, not in and not out. It's kind of where the church of the living God is in the book of Revelation, the Church of Laodicea. They are described as lukewarm, tepid, not hot, not cold. A much better picture is to say they were a church sitting on the fence. You know, God doesn't want people on the fence. He wants you to make up your mind about where you're going to stand, where you're going to live, and what you're going to do. He doesn't want a church that's lukewarm: half hot and half cold. He really wants you to be a person who says, "I've made up my mind, and this is the route I'm going to take."

Our Serious Need To Change
Take a look at your life, peer, peep, and peruse the confines of your own human existence. Ask yourself this question: am I really all in when it regards Jesus? Am I 100% in the faith? Do I really follow the Lord, or am I sitting on the fence- halfway in and halfway out? God says today, "I want you to make up your mind about what you're going to do and do it with great fervor and great passion." After all, sitting on the fence makes everyone uncomfortable, even you.

Our Sincere Petition
Lord, today is a day I want You to know that my mind is sincerely made up about who You are, what You are, and what You have to offer me. I love You because You loved me first, and, Lord, I seek to follow You in faith until the day I die. I pray these petitions. In The Name of Jesus, Amen.

WEEK 11: The Answer is Knocking
Day 7

God's Word For You Today: TRUST ME; HE'S NOT SOLICITING

Our Scripture

As many as I love, I rebuke and chasten: be zealous therefore, and repent. Behold, I stand at the door, and knock: if any man hear my voice, and open the door, I will come in to him, and will sup with him, and he with me (Rev. 3:19-20, KJV).

Our Simple Lesson

I used to carry mail for the United States Postal Service when I was in college. It was a great part-time job. I was a casual carrier. And as I would carry mail, I hated the day that we had advos. Advos were advertisements that had to go to every house on the street, every home in the neighborhood. It was the most incredulous day, and I hated it. But I couldn't help but take notice of the fact that while delivering my mail, there were signs on the door of some of the houses on my route that read "No soliciting." When you read the words, "Behold, I stand at the door and knock," oftentimes we treat God like He's soliciting, like He's begging, like He's really trying to knock so that you will have to answer because He is getting on your nerves. The truth of the matter is, He's not soliciting. Grace in action? Yes. Mercy in motion? Of course. Soliciting? Absolutely not. To receive the Lord in repentance is a blessing for you. The benefit is for us. The big idea suggests that at least He cares enough to knock.

Our Serious Need To Change

Today is a day of decision-making for you, as every day and each day is. Each day, you make decisions to do certain things and not to do certain things anymore. Today, I would like for you to make a three-bulleted list of some things that you choose not to do anymore, some things that you're going to make an about-face on, to repent from, and to start a new journey with God that's deeper, more meaningful and more productive.

Our Sincere Petition

God, there are areas of my life where I see my own weaknesses. Today, I would pray that You will give me the strength to make changes that are needed and necessary. Where I am weak, You make me strong. And, God, if You're not going to make me strong, then please be my strength.

In The Name of Jesus, Amen.

WEEK 11: The Answer is Knocking
Week 11 Conclusion

HIGHER THAN THE TOP
HT3

Life Application

God's word to the church of today does not seem to be a word that gives you great prosperity. It's not a word that suggests that you ought to be praying for wealth, riches, and earthly fame. The word to the church of today is "repent." You don't hear it much. Yet the message for you today from the Master and Lord of His own people is, change your mind, change your direction, change how you pray, shift how you worship, bow your knee, and go another direction because sitting on the fence, being lukewarm, does not please God.

If being lukewarm does not please God, being on fire for the Him makes Him happy. With this in mind, consider taking your faith higher than the top by helping your Church family fulfill the Great Commission. Make a list of five people that you know need God in a special way. Cover them in prayer and invite them to attend a worship service with you. Follow up with them to personally ask them if they would be willing to join you in living Christ.

In short, do the work of an evangelist!

WEEK 12: But What Do You Say

Day 1

God's Word For You Today: EVERYBODY HAS AN OPINION, I WANT TO KNOW YOURS

Our Scripture
When Jesus came into the coasts of Caesarea Philippi, he asked his disciples, saying, Whom do men say that I the Son of man am (St. Matt. 16:13, KJV)?

Our Simple Lesson
You live in the age of social media critics and opinions from everybody. If you want to see a quick debate surface, simply go to any social media site of your choosing, Facebook, TikTok, Twitter, Instagram, or Snapchat, and just begin reading the comments of other people about certain posts. It's because everybody has an opinion. But here is one thing I'm sure of, not every opinion really matters. People will always have something to say. There will always be a critic, a negativist, a pessimist, and perhaps even an antagonist. But here is the real truth: everybody may have an opinion, but sometimes only certain opinions really matter.

Jesus, in your study passage for the week, is in a place called Caesarea, Philippi. He is about to begin revealing who He is to His disciples. They are about to know Him in a way they've never known Him before. He poses a question that simply asks, "Whom do men say that I, the Son of man, am?" In short, what He's saying is that everybody has an opinion, but I want to know yours.

Our Serious Need To Change
What's your real opinion of Jesus? How do you really feel about Him? Don't be so quick to answer. How you see Him is ultimately how you will treat Him. Think about your answer. Be candid and transparent about what you really think of Him and who He is for you. Your honest answer has eternal consequences.

Our Sincere Petition
Lord, thank You for showing me how great You really are. I have always known You to be present, but I haven't always walked with You like I'm walking right now. Closer, O God, to Thee is my sincere desire.

In The Name of Jesus, Amen.

WEEK 12: But What Do You Say

Day 2

God's Word For You Today: HE SAY, SHE SAY, THEY SAY, HEARSAY

Our Scripture
When Jesus came into the coasts of Caesarea Philippi, he asked his disciples, saying, Whom do men say that I the Son of man am (St. Matt. 16:13, KJV)?

Our Simple Lesson
There are times that you can get called into public opinion and discussions, and you hear words like, he say, she say, they say. Well, isn't that hearsay? The truth of the matter is that none of this really matters. It is really what you say and what God has to say. In our Scripture lesson this week, the Lord pulls on the hearts of His disciples regarding a matter of public opinion. *"Who do men say that I, the Son of Man, am?"* The disciples answer by saying, "….some say you're Isaiah, Jeremiah, one of the prophets." But He says, "…what I really want to know is what you have to say." It is because what he say, she say, they say, and hearsay doesn't matter, but what you say does. Your life in Christ Jesus is wrapped within it.

Our Serious Need To Change
When I was younger, I saw God as my father in the pulpit, in the robe, preaching to me. Thank God that view changed. My dad needed a redeemer, too. When I got older, I saw God as the God of the big blue sky. But that changed when it rained on me one day, and I discovered that sometimes blue skies can become black clouds. As I've gotten older, I see God in different ways. My view of God has shifted and changed over the years. How do you see God right now? Understand this: how you see Him will really determine what your service to Him looks like. If you see God as small and minuscule, weak and sorry, you will treat God that same way. But if you see God as mighty and powerful, enthroned and sovereign, you will treat Him like you see Him. And there are times when how you see God will cause you to change your mind about Him and treat Him differently. It's repentance at its best.

Our Sincere Petition
Thank You for revealing Yourself to me, O God. Thank You for the growth in how I see You. Today, I am happy to announce that I see You as my Savior who rescued me from sin, one who would redeem me at the cross, one who would go to hell on my behalf and be resurrected three days later. O how excellent is my God in all the Earth. In The Name of Jesus, Amen.

WEEK 12: But What Do You Say

Day 3

God's Word For You Today: THIS POP QUIZ ONLY HAS ONE QUESTION ON IT

Our Scripture

When Jesus came into the coasts of Caesarea Philippi, he asked his disciples, saying, Whom do men say that I the Son of man am (St. Matt. 16:13, KJV)?

Our Simple Lesson

I didn't mind taking tests in school, especially if they were announced or on a syllabus. I mean, after all, it was a test that you knew you had to take. Whether it was a midterm test, a final exam, or a test that was comprehensive, I would find myself working hard gathering notes to make sure I could pass those tests to perform satisfactorily, if you will. But the test that got the most of me every time was the dreaded pop quiz. It was a day that would cause my blood pressure to rise and perspiration to fall from various parts of my physiological anatomy. I always hated a pop quiz. You'd walk into class and hear the teacher make an announcement that sounded like this, "Clear your desk and take out one sheet of paper and something to write with." "Oh no, not that," I would say.

Today, as you study your Scripture lesson, Jesus gives His disciples a pop quiz. He only asked one question, so either you would make 100 or a flat 0. *Who do men say that I the Son of man am*? That's the question. And in this one question, the one answer puts you in Heaven or hell. The one answer blesses or curses your future. The one answer saves you or literally puts you in a place where there is no hope and no help.

Our Serious Need To Change

So here's your pop quiz for the day. Who is Jesus for you? The answer to this means everything. Choose wisely, for He is King of kings and Lord of lords.

Our Sincere Petition

Father, I stretch my hands to Thee. No other help I know. If I withdraw myself from Thee, whither shall I go? I have no hope but You, O God. Thank You for saving me. Thank You for healing me. Thank You for letting me pass the pop quiz. You are my Lord, my Savior, my God, and my Guide.

In The Name of Jesus, Amen.

WEEK 12: But What Do You Say
Day 4

God's Word For You Today: IF YOU DON'T KNOW, NOW YOU KNOW

Our Scripture
When Jesus came into the coasts of Caesarea Philippi, he asked his disciples, saying, Whom do men say that I the Son of man am (St. Matt. 16:13, KJV)?

Our Simple Lesson
I want you to read this particular devotional with an open mind. I, too, like the rest of you, have areas of my life where I'm making some necessary changes. So, with that in mind, I want to be transparent. I still love music. I love jazz. I love R & B. I love hip-hop. I love rap. I know you can't see it, and that's good. It just means that God is still working on me. Okay, a moment of total transparency: I still like Tupac and listen to a little Biggie Smalls every now and then. I love how Biggie would sample music from the past to make music for the present. On one occasion, he sampled some music from the Isley Brothers, and his ending phrase that became the mantra in the music industry was a phrase that simply said, "If you don't know, now you know."

When you begin dealing with this passage that you're studying for the week, Jesus asks the question, "*Who do men say that I the Son of man am?*" The Spirit of the Lord moves upon Simon Peter, and he openly declares, "Thou art the Christ, Son of the living God. Jesus' answer was like this. "Flesh and blood hath not revealed this to you, Peter." In other words, you didn't get the answer from your mother or your father. This one came from God.

Our Serious Need To Change
Once you know, you can never not know. Once you know who He is for you and your journey, that will never change. Thank God for those of you reading this devotional who can say, Pastor, I may not be perfect, but I know.

Our Sincere Petition
Today, O God, I pray to You because I know. I offer my supplications to You because I know. I know my Redeemer lives. I know my Lord reigns. I know my God rules, and I know that my God has a name that is above every name.

In The Name of Jesus, Amen.

WEEK 12: But What Do You Say
Day 5

God's Word For You Today: CHANGE HAPPENS WHEN YOUR MIND SHIFTS

Our Scripture
When Jesus came into the coasts of Caesarea Philippi, he asked his disciples, saying, Whom do men say that I the Son of man am (St. Matt. 16:13, KJV)?

Our Simple Lesson
The disciples, who were following Jesus, were not bad men. They were common everyday men. In short, they were good guys, but they never quite saw the Lord for who He really was. They were near Him but did not know Him. As they walked with Him, they were there to see things that should have changed their minds instantly. When Jesus calmed the raging sea, when He spoke the words "Peace be still," when He came walking on the sea and transformed water molecules into a cement sidewalk, when He took two fish and five barley loaves and fed 5000 people and gave each of them a basket full of bread, surely it should have shifted their minds.

You see, change happens when your mind shifts, when you see things differently, when you see God differently, when you see yourself, your sin, and your salvation differently. It's all about your mind and how things shift when it changes.

Our Serious Need To Change
When your mind changes, it is like the rudder of a ship. Everything around you shifts for the better in the direction you're headed in or for the worse in a negative light; the decision is yours. Here's my advice: make the decisions that will bless you in the end. You will never live to regret it. If you haven't already, make a decision for Jesus. There is no one like Him on Earth or, for that matter, in Heaven.

Our Sincere Petition
O Lord, my Lord, I choose You today. I choose You in my life, in my walk, in my witness, in my warfare, and in my work. I choose You in my wealth. My prayer is that You would grant me mercy for my failures and grace for mishaps. Thank You for being who You are in my life.

In The Name of Jesus, Amen.

WEEK 12: But What Do You Say
DAY 6

God's Word For You Today: THE HOLY GHOST GETS THE GLORY FOR THIS ONE

Our Scripture
When Jesus came into the coasts of Caesarea Philippi, he asked his disciples, saying, Whom do men say that I the Son of man am (St. Matt. 16:13, KJV).

Our Simple Lesson
Many times, you are quick to take the credit for things. Statements like I did it, I made it, I bought it, I won it, and I achieved it become commonplace. It's the personal pronoun "I" that can become so arrogant, so self-conceited, so self-aggrandized. Still, when you realize that the person who gets the credit for what God does in your life is God Himself, it is then, and only then, you will have to admit that the Father in Heaven receives the glory for the things God has done in your life.

It is what takes place in this narrative as you study this week. When Peter admits openly that Jesus is The Christ, He says, "Thou art the Christ, Son of the living God," Jesus lets Peter know that flesh and blood did not reveal this to him, but that wisdom came from God the Father, who resides in Heaven. In short, Peter was right, but he will never be able to take credit for what God the Father did in his life. God alone gets the glory!

Our Serious Need To Change
Take a moment and ask yourself this question: in what way do you make sure God gets the glory for the things He has done in your life, including the changes you have made that have been necessary? Be honest with your answer.

Our Sincere Petition
Today, O God, I give You glory. At this moment, O Lord, my glory that You've given me, any fame, any pomp, any circumstance, any blessing, any accolades that You've bestowed upon me, I pause right now to say to You in my private petitions, to God be the glory for every door You've opened, for every way You've made.

In The Name of Jesus, Amen.

WEEK 12: But What Do You Say
Day 7

God's Word For You Today: THE REAL CHANGE AGENT IS GOD

Our Scripture
When Jesus came into the coasts of Caesarea Philippi, he asked his disciples, saying, Whom do men say that I the Son of man am (St. Matt. 16:13, KJV).

Our Simple Lesson
As we finish this week of study, looking intently at Matthew 16:13, we must conclude that the real change agent in our lives is God. If the Lord is the one who wakes us, leads us, guides us, and provides for us, then ultimately, He is the one who can claim victory for the changes that we make. Wait, God does not impede upon or shift human thought or volition, but like a kite in the wind, He can influence it. The influences that are around a kite determine the height of the kite and the direction it will travel.

Thank God today for the true inspiration that He provides because that inspiration changes the course of your life in radical ways. He inspires us with His love. He inspires us with His mercy. He inspires us with His grace. He inspires us with information that comes from the revelation of His Word. God's inspiration is the real change agent in every change we will ever make.

Our Serious Need To Change
In what ways has God inspired you? In what seasons have those inspirations been the greatest? Has He ever opened a door for you that you did not want to walk through, but when you walked through it, the blessing of the Lord fell in your lap? Have you ever had a season of your life where you were not happy about the direction you were going in, and God gave you a chance to change? It was because the inspiration and change agent behind the whole thing was God Himself.

Our Sincere Petition
Inspire me, O God, please, for Your sake and for Your glory in the life that You've given me to live. Let my true inspiration come only from You.

In The Name of Jesus, Amen.

WEEK 12: But What Do You Say
Week 12 Conclusion

HIGHER THAN THE TOP
HT3

Life Application

One believer who knows who Jesus is can change a home, a neighborhood, a city, a county, a state, a country, and the world—just one Christian. Imagine for a moment what a congregation of Christians, a cluster, if you will, all willing to tell the world who He really is, could do, perhaps influence. Here is the truth: He is the Christ, the Anointed One, the Promised Son of David, the Messiah, the One who for us would be God wrapped in a human body, placed, positioned in purpose for the redemption of humankind. That is the God we serve. His inspiration for our lives is to press us to move forward in the faith like never before.

That is why it is so important for you to belong to a congregation of Christians who will help take your love for God, your worship for God, and your service to God higher than the top. Consider how much time you spend with God in private and intentionally increase it. Think about how much time you spend helping others and do even more of it. Look at your financial giving to your local church and make a decision to give more.

Do something for Him that would make your life a witness to the fact that nobody can do it like your King can.

WEEK 13: Trying to Fix it By Yourself can Kill You

Day 1

God's Word For You Today: JUDAS WASN'T A BAD GUY

Our Scripture
Then Judas, which had betrayed him, when he saw that he was condemned, repented himself, and brought again the thirty pieces of silver to the chief priests and elders (St. Matt. 27:3, KJV).

Our Simple Lesson
Some people on Earth are just bad people. They do evil, harmful, hateful, heinous things to other people. But some people do bad things that are really good people. Such is the case with Judas. You are going to be studying him this week.

Judas Iscariot was one of the Lord's disciples who decided he would help Jesus start a war. He was sick of the Roman government being over his people. He knew Jesus had the power to calm a raging sea and raise a dead man back to life. So, he concluded he could use the power of Jesus Christ for self-aggrandizement, start a war, and, with Jesus on his side, win. Not bad, right?

When you read the story of Judas, here is what you will discover: he felt bad about the sin he committed. The Bible said he repented himself. It means he felt sorry in this text. But feeling sorry for sin is not enough. Godly sorrow for personal sins is where it begins, but it is not where it ends. Repentance, if it is going to be holistic, involves not just feeling sorry for your past sins but making the changes that lead to righteousness.

Our Serious Need To Change
To feel sorry about sins is one thing, but making the necessary changes with Jesus Christ is another. As you spend this devotional time with God take a moment and survey the landscape of your own soul. Ask yourself this question, what changes do I really need to make?

Our Sincere Petition
So, God, I pray today for the strength to make changes that may not be pleasing in Your sight. God, I give you full permission and a free recourse. Make those changes in my life that are needed and necessary for me to completely please You and to live out the destiny You have already prearranged for my human existence on Earth.

In The Name of Jesus, Amen.

WEEK 13: Trying to Fix it By Yourself can Kill You

Day 2

God's Word For You Today: THE ONE PROBLEM YOU WILL NEVER BE ABLE TO FIX

Our Scripture
Then Judas, which had betrayed him, when he saw that he was condemned, repented himself, and brought again the thirty pieces of silver to the chief priests and elders (St. Matt. 27:3, KJV).

Our Simple Lesson
There are some problems in your life you, with the help of God and human volition, can fix. But there are some problems you will never be able to address or repair. Only God can address those issues. Your sin is one of those things. No matter how badly you feel about your sin, how much you wash yourself, and how many times you fast and pray, you will never be able to fix the problem of human sin. If you could fix your sin, you would be God. It's why you need God in your life because He alone addresses the issue of sin. Judas has sinned against God. In your study passage today, he betrays Jesus for thirty pieces of silver. Don't feel too bad for Judas because Peter denied Him for free. The truth of the matter is all of us betray God when we sin. The text says Judas repented himself, and he brought the thirty pieces of silver back to the people who gave it to him in the first place, who were religious but completely lost. The mistake Judas made was trying to offer a refund for his own sins. When silver could not pay for it, it would require the blood of a crucified lamb. That is the only way to fix it: the blood of the lamb.

Our Serious Need To Change
No matter how much you want to fix yourself, you cannot. You can only come out with self-aggrandized change and transition, but you'll never fix the real issue, which is sin. It is why repentance has to be understood in the right light. To feel sorry for your sins is necessary, but to make the changes from the sin is a divine requirement. Make the changes that are necessary and leave the glory for God. He deserves it.

Our Sincere Petition
Bless the Lord, O my soul, and all that's within me, bless His holy name. Today, O God, I am grateful that I am unable and inept to fix my sin. I praise Your name because You alone fixed it at the cross. Thank You, Jesus, for a vacant cross, an empty tomb, and an occupied throne in Heaven.

In The Name of Jesus, Amen.

WEEK 13: Trying to Fix it By Yourself can Kill You
Day 3

God's Word For You Today: REFUSE TO BE A SELL-OUT

Our Scripture
Then Judas, which had betrayed him, when he saw that he was condemned, repented himself, and brought again the thirty pieces of silver to the chief priests and elders (St. Matt. 27:3, KJV).

Our Simple Lesson
You live in a culture where you watch people sell out all the time. It's normal. If the Cowboys are winning, people are wearing jerseys that are not even fans, and we hear you say things like, "We won." But if the Cowboys lose long enough, some of those same people will take their jerseys off and burn them and say, "I'm through with those Cowboys." They are just sellouts.

When it comes to walking with God, what Judas does in your study passage this week is sell Him out. He sold Him for thirty pieces of silver. He literally did the unthinkable. He goes to the temple, asks for money, gets the money, and tries to fix it by giving the money back. You see, here's the truth: if you're a sellout, you're simply a sellout.

Our Serious Need To Change
Here's a good devotional question to ask on a day like today: in what ways are you a sellout? In what ways have you sold God short? The real truth of the matter is that to sell God short means to sell yourself even shorter. The reason Jesus would die on the cross, bleed, suffer the death of a criminal in public, go to hell, pay out your lease, and get up three days later is because what God sees in you is someone worth dying for.

Our Sincere Petition
Lord, I may be a lot of things, but I refuse to be a sellout. In areas of my life where I am totally committed to You, build more strength. God, in portions and pieces of my fragmented human existence, take what looks weak and make it strong. O God, in those places where I just cannot do any better, please know that I'm anything but a sellout. I'm a saint that's still under construction.

In The Name of Jesus, Amen.

WEEK 13: Trying to Fix it By Yourself can Kill You

Day 4

God's Word For You Today: HOW MUCH DOES YOUR CHRIST COST

Our Scripture
Then Judas, which had betrayed him, when he saw that he was condemned, repented himself, and brought again the thirty pieces of silver to the chief priests and elders (St. Matt. 27:3, KJV).

Our Simple Lesson
You live in a consumer-based generation. Thanks to Amazon, you no longer have to go to a brick-and-mortar store. You can just sit at the house, click, and make an order. We live in a culture where people buy things at the speed of light. You literally move quickly. Debit cards and credit cards are in hand. You are looking at items that appear extraordinary on the screen, and without hesitation or reservation, you use PayPal. You use any form of payment you can put your hands on, and you get what you think you have paid for. It's because you measure the cost, and you buy the items.

You know, when you read a verse in the Bible like the one you've been studying, where Judas literally accepts thirty pieces of silver for the life of Jesus, it makes you ponder the inquiry, how much does your Christ cost? How much does it cost you to turn your back on God? How much does it cost for you to say, "hey, Jesus, this is what You're worth to me?" The good news is that His value system of you is not your value system of Him.

Our Serious Need To Change
When the Lord considered how much He would pay for you, He did not put a down payment on the item. He did not pick you up from a sale rack or a clearance bar in the back of a store. He paid the price in full. The Lord saw your value and decided to give His life so that you might have a life to live.

Our Sincere Petition
O God, just as You laid Your life down for me, I make a decision right now in prayer to lay my life down for You. Today, O God, I see repentance as restoration because You have restored me to the place where I am willing to give You my life, not in pieces, not in patches, and not in portions. But, God, today, I want You to have all of me.

In The Name of Jesus, Amen.

WEEK 13: Trying to Fix it By Yourself can Kill You
Day 5

God's Word For You Today: TURN TO GOD

Our Scripture
Then Judas, which had betrayed him, when he saw that he was condemned, repented himself, and brought again the thirty pieces of silver to the chief priests and elders (St. Matt. 27:3, KJV).

Our Simple Lesson
There is one thing that I want you to leave this lesson passage with that you've been studying all week long, and that is this: when you have failed, faltered, sinned, made mistakes, come across bad habits that you can't seem to get rid of, or even have personal, private issues of struggle, do not turn inwardly to yourself. Don't try to fix it yourself. Do not turn outwardly to other people. They have their own struggles to deal with. Turn to God. Turn to Him.

The difference between Peter's denial and Judas' betrayal is that Judas turned inwardly and repented, trying to fix his brokenness himself. My friends, you are not qualified to repair you, but God is. The problem with modern-day Christianity is that we keep taking our lives to shade-tree mechanics who don't qualify to do the work. Give your life to God, and I promise you, He can do with you what you could never do with yourself.

Our Serious Need To Change
If you have not presented your body to God as a living sacrifice, then my word of wisdom for today is to do it and do it now. Turn to God. He's waiting for you.

Our Sincere Petition
Lord Jesus, I give myself to You again at this very moment. It's not as if I've never done it before, but today, I feel a sincere sense of urgency to tell You, in places where I'm broken, I need You. In spaces where I'm fractured, I desire You, and in places, O God, where I have failed miserably, I need You most of all. Thank You, Lord, for opening Your heart to me because on days like today, when I look carefully at myself, I need You more than ever before.

In The Name of Jesus, Amen.

WEEK 13: Trying to Fix it By Yourself can Kill You

Day 6

God's Word For You Today: DON'T LET THE MISTAKES OF YOUR PAST ERASE THE BLESSING OF YOUR FUTURE

Our Scripture
Then Judas, which had betrayed him, when he saw that he was condemned, repented himself, and brought again the thirty pieces of silver to the chief priests and elders (St. Matt. 27:3, KJV).

Our Simple Lesson
One of the saddest stories in the Bible is the one we are studying this week. In the complete narrative of Judas Iscariot, he is one of the Lord's disciples, handpicked by the Messiah, one of the initial twelve, who literally commits suicide. Judas, as the scripture defines it, went and hung himself. It is a tragedy. It is one of the most hurtful narratives ever. The end result, however, is that he tried to fix his own sin. After feeling sorry about what he had done, he tried his best, took his problems into his own hands, and discovered his hands were not big enough to handle them.

Our Serious Need To Change
In what ways have you discovered that your problems are too big for your hands to handle? The word of caution and the word of wisdom today in your study time of repentance is this: don't let the mistakes of your past erase the blessing of your future. God is a God of redemption and restoration. He is a God of another chance. And no matter how bad it may seem, what is too big for your hands is always just right for Him. To repent means to feel sorry about your sin and to make changes. Going to God is the best decision for your future.

Our Sincere Petition
Merciful Master, I want my life in Your hands. Most importantly, I want my mistakes in Your hands. I want my sins in Your hands. I want my human struggle in Your hands. The reason I want them in Your hands is because no hand on Earth has a nail in it for me like Yours does. Thank You, Lord, for the cross.

In The Name of Jesus, Amen.

WEEK 13: Trying to Fix it By Yourself can Kill You
Day 7

God's Word For You Today: REPENTANCE SAYS HE CAN FIX IT

Our Scripture
Then Judas, which had betrayed him, when he saw that he was condemned, repented himself, and brought again the thirty pieces of silver to the chief priests and elders (St. Matt. 27:3, KJV).

Our Simple Lesson
Judas is the Lord's disciple who repented, but he did it unto himself. He tried to change himself. He tried to fix his own mistakes, his own mishaps. It sounds so responsible, but actually, it's horrible because no one on Earth is trained and can help you with past mistakes, present struggles, and personal demons like God can. Repentance, in a nutshell, says, "God alone can fix it." It's what God wants. It is what worship is. Worship is you living for God in your body and giving God your undivided commitment. Repentance is simply you saying to God, "Lord, give me the strength to make the change so that the change I make pleases the God who helped me to make it." Repentance is fruit for the soul. It is a life-changing moment where you realize that what's broken in your life can only be fixed, repaired, addressed, restored, and renewed by the God who wakes you up every morning.

Our Serious Need To Change
From time to time in your life, feelings of helplessness and hopelessness can arise. When you look at yourself carefully and closely, there are changes in your life that seemingly never get any better. Have you been there before? And then there were times when you can honestly say, God changed this for me. I don't even know what day it happened. It was gradual. It may have even been subtle, but whatever the case is, you can testify that it wasn't your strength or your doing. Someone greater than you did it. That's what repentance really is, a turning to God that says, I knew He could do it, even when I couldn't. It is the saving grace of God that says I can't save me, but God, You can.

Our Sincere Petition
Lord, today I am made aware of the fact that it's been You all along. Forgive me for getting in Your way and trying to fix myself, and forgive me, O God, for being an impediment to my own spiritual progress. But today, thank You for the changes you have made in my life and thank You for the repentance and restoration, the redemption and renewal that is mine by faith.
In The Name of Jesus, Amen.

WEEK 13: Trying to Fix it By Yourself can Kill You
Week 13 Conclusion

HIGHER THAN THE TOP
HT3

Life Application

Serving the Lord in a local assembly can be difficult. It can be both bothersome and frustrating. However, today, if you are going to take faith higher than the top, I want to exhort you, empower you, and encourage you to get past people: what they say and what they think. I want you to get to a place where you take your brokenness, your bitterness, and the things that bother you straight to God. And then tell God that while you work on me, I will work for You. It's a very beautiful swap and trade. God works on you while you work for Him. And while you work for Him, God works on you.

You will always run into people who are narrow-minded, who will tell you things like you should go sit down until God is finished working on you because you are a complete mess. But the truth of the matter is your mess is in the Master's hands, and while you work for Him, He is still working on you until the day He is finished with His work, and He calls you from labor to reward. Repentance says, God, work on me. And I don't want You to just work on me; make room for me to work for You.

WEEK 14: They Wouldn't, So He Didn't

Day 1

God's Word For You Today: SOMEBODY IS IN TROUBLE, AND I DON'T WANT IT TO BE ME

Our Scripture
Then began he to upbraid the cities wherein most of his mighty works were done, because they repented not (St. Matt. 11:20, KJV).

Our Simple Lesson
I'll never forget the day I heard the front door close. I could tell by the movement of my mother's feet that someone was in trouble. I just did not want it to be me. When my mother walked in, she simply asked the question, "Who ate the candy that was in the pantry?" Silence filled the room as she surveyed the surroundings. She walked into her bedroom and came out with a belt in her hand. All I knew was that I was not the one who had done it, and I was certain that someone was in trouble, and it would not be me. In your study passage for the week, you see the woes that Jesus offers cities like Chorazon and Bethsaida. These are places where people did not repent. The passage says, "because they repented not, He did not do miracles there." He did not favor them with a presence that would cause extraordinary miraculous occurrences to take place because they repented not. In short, they were in trouble. You will never find God being angry with a sinner who knows he's a sinner. The Lord has issues with religious people whose holiness is of themselves and who refuse to repent.

Our Serious Need To Change
Are there moments in your life where you really go to God and just tell God, I'm sorry? If you haven't done it in a while, every now and then, you should do it. If you have not shared this kind of intimacy with God lately why not do it right now? Whisper these words to God, "Lord I'm sorry." They give honor to God and they bless you.

Our Sincere Petition
Lord, it is at this time in my journey with You that I realize that being unrepentant could cause You to become angry with me. Jesus, I do realize there are those on Earth who will be in trouble with You one day. Please know I do not want to be one of them. God, more personally, please forgive me for my sins. I repent of anything that will separate You and me.

In The Name of Jesus, Amen.

WEEK 14: They Wouldn't, So He Didn't
Day 2

God's Word For You Today: THERE'S A REASON WHY RELIGIOUS PEOPLE DON'T REPENT

Our Scripture
Then began he to upbraid the cities wherein most of his mighty works were done, because they repented not (St. Matt. 11:20, KJV).

Our Simple Lesson
In your study passage this week, you find a group of religious people. They practice praying. They believe in worshiping. They exist in cities where God is held in high esteem. The problem is they don't repent. The very last phrase of verse 20 in Chapter 11 reads like this: "...*because they repented not.*" They felt no sorrow for their sins. They felt no need to change. And it is here you find the most significant problem. Religious people never repent.

Here is why - because a religious person looks at their lives and says, look how good I am. "Look at how great I am. Look at how many mistakes I don't make. Look at how holy I am. Look at the righteousness I possess." Their lenses are warped. Their views of themselves are that the sinners are other people and not the man in the mirror. Here is the truth: all have sinned and come short of the glory of God, even the most religious elite.

Our Serious Need To Change
I was asked one day if I preached "holiness" as a practice from my pulpit. Here is what I answered: I preached the gospel from my pulpit, and the gospel shows us holiness, not in the actions of our people, but in the grace of our God. No one does it right all the time, no matter how holy you may think yourself to be. Holiness is a gift from God. It is the fruit that comes from the root of His grace, which is still amazing. It's why religious people don't repent.

Our Sincere Petition
So today, O God, I thank You for a relationship that allows me to repent on a regular basis, and I celebrate the holiness You have given to me, and I am thankful for the sins that no longer befall me. How grateful I am for addictions that no longer have me bound, and I celebrate even those changes You are yet to make.

In The Name of Jesus, Amen.

WEEK 14: They Wouldn't, So He Didn't
Day 3

God's Word For You Today: PRACTICE DOES NOT ALWAYS MAKE PERFECT

Our Scripture
Then began he to upbraid the cities wherein most of his mighty works were done, because they repented not (St. Matt. 11:20, KJV).

Our Simple Lesson
There are some clichés that you hear that sound good, but they don't fare well when you try to practice them. One of those is a small piece that says, "Practice makes perfect." Here's the truth: that's not always the truth. Practice does not always make one perfect. You know that because you can practice a religion wrong, and it's still bad even though you practice it. Jesus warns that the precepts and principles of these people are good practices. They practice prayer; that's a good practice. They practice worship; that's a good practice. They practice looking righteous on the outside, even though their hearts are corrupt on the inside. They practice it, but it doesn't make them perfect. What makes the Christian perfect is not human perfection produced. It's divine perfection that's been presented and received. Our holiness in God comes from God and not us. The blessing of today is knowing that God will produce it with our belief and faith in Him. The trouble with the religious people in this passage is that they never repent because they never see a need to.

Our Serious Need To Change
If you've ever been around real religious people, they'll remind you of why Jesus really died on the cross. It was not only for sinners who knew they were sinners; it was for religious people who had no idea that their lifestyle was foul before God. Today, examine your heart and move religion out of the way. It's a practice. It's a precept. It's only a principle; it's a dogma. It's a doctrine. Get to a place where you have a relationship where you can say, "What a friend I have in Jesus. All of my sins and grieves to bear." Pray, not just to practice it. Pray because you want to talk with God, and you want God to speak with you. Worship, not so that it can be exciting. Worship so that you can tell God how much you love Him and how much you desire to please Him. There's a difference between these, and my prayer is that you'd find it.

WEEK 14: They Wouldn't, So He Didn't

Our Sincere Petition

Eternal God, my Father, today I desire a relationship with You more profound and more meaningful than I've ever had before in my life, granted by way of Your grace.

In The Name of Jesus, Amen.

WEEK 14: They Wouldn't, So He Didn't
Day 4

God's Word For You Today: IT'S NOT A COMMAND, IT'S A SUGGESTION

Our Scripture
Then began he to upbraid the cities wherein most of his mighty works were done, because they repented not (St. Matt. 11:20, KJV).

Our Simple Lesson
You have often heard that God gives commands and not suggestions. But here's another look at that same thought. There were times when God gave suggestions, but they were not commands. When you are told to repent, it's not a command. The choice is yours. You can repent, or you can choose not to. The decision is yours, and God permits and allows it.

The people in the passage that you're learning from this week choose not to. Here is what's interesting: God doesn't go back and make up their minds for them. He doesn't even change their minds. He leaves them in their condition. It is also why the Lord chose not to do miracles in their presence. It's not like Jesus is not a miracle worker. It's just that the unrepentant soul is not worthy of the favor of seeing what miracles really look like.

Our Serious Need To Change
It is possible that your unbelief could hinder what God really wants to do for you. Unrepentant sins in your life could cause the hand of favor to be removed from you. If you're wise, you should just simply make repentance and a constant consciousness of human sin and flaws evident in your everyday walk and witness. It's worth it because you never completely measure up. So, just in case there is a sin in your life, ask God to remove it. It's not just forgiveness. It's repentance when the action follows the petition.

Our Sincere Petition
And so today, Lord, I pray in the name of Jesus that You would simply move anything in my life that's not like You. It's my prayer. It's my plea. It's my sacred supplication and my petition.

In The Name of Jesus, Amen.

WEEK 14: They Wouldn't, So He Didn't
Day 5

God's Word For You Today: "TO BE OR NOT TO BE" IS NOT THE REAL QUESTION

Our Scripture
Then began he to upbraid the cities wherein most of his mighty works were done, because they repented not (St. Matt. 11:20, KJV).

Our Simple Lesson
It happens in Act 3, Scene 1 of the Shakespearean drama "Hamlet" where Hamlet, in a soliloquy, begins to look inwardly and poses an interesting interrogative for himself to grapple with. He says, "To be or not to be. That is the question." The real truth of the matter is, after careful examination through the lenses of repentance, "to be or not to be" is not the real question. "To repent or not to repent" is.

You see, the real truth of the matter is that the Lord gives you the opportunity for change. He presents ways for you to shift from the way of life that you have lived in the past to a way of life that says, turn to me. Come back to me. Make an about-face. A U-turn is allowed. The truth of the matter is to be or not to be is not the question. It's the answer. Just to still be alive means that you have room to make shifts, changes, and adjustments that have divine consequences and eternal consequences attached to them. Make decisions that will bless you today.

Our Serious Need To Change
While Hamlet wrestles with "to be or not to be," your wrestle may be slightly different; it's to change or not to change, and the choice is yours. To be is a blessing. To change is the benefit. My word of wisdom for you today is to take the benefit and the blessing. Move forward and hold God's hand while He makes the changes in your life He needs to make to produce the redemptive perfection He will let rest upon you that really belongs to Him.

Our Sincere Petition
God, thank You today for letting me still be alive. To be able to read this devotional, understand what's printed, and receive it by faith says I still exist. My being is still here. Thank You for the changes You're making in my life. I trust that You will make them to please Yourself so that it's for Your glory and my good.

In The Name of Jesus, Amen.

WEEK 14: They Wouldn't, So He Didn't
Day 6

God's Word For You Today: IF YOU DON'T, GOD WON'T

Our Scripture
Then began he to upbraid the cities wherein most of his mighty works were done, because they repented not (St. Matt. 11:20, KJV).

Our Simple Lesson
The Lord Jesus Christ, throughout the scriptures, is a miracle worker. He is a life changer. He opens blinded eyes. He heals wounded hearts. He makes lame men walk, deaf men hear, and weak people gain strength. He turns water into wine. He allows a hemorrhaging woman to touch the hem of His garment and be made whole. He takes dead people and brings them back to life. He calms raging seas. He is God in a body. Yet, there is a space in the text that's rather disturbing. As you've studied this passage this week, it's alarming to read the words that most of the mighty works were done there. But He stopped doing these works because the people wouldn't repent. You know, perhaps that's why you don't see as many miracles today as you did when you read the scriptures. We're living in a culture of the church where saints don't repent anymore. I looked through my sermon dossier to realize that I only had two sermons on the subject of repentance over nearly 30 years of preaching. It's why you're reading this book right now. It's because I believe the key to living in the lap of God is a humility-filled believer who understands the beauty and bounty of repentance.

Our Serious Need To Change
Take a moment as you spend this devotional time with God. Take a proverbial broom. Sweep around your own front door. Don't stop at the door. Clean out your closet. Deal with the dirty window seals of how you see your realities. Check out the hidden places and the junk drawer that you have. Fix it and tell God, it's because You've brought me to a place of repentance that I'm able to make these changes.

Our Sincere Petition
Thank You, Jesus, for the necessary change in my life. Thank You, oh God, for the U-turns that have been needed. Thank You for mercy, which I could not live without.

In The Name of Jesus, Amen.

WEEK 14: They Wouldn't, So He Didn't
Day 7

God's Word For You Today: IT'S HARD BUT FAIR, SAD BUT TRUE

Our Scripture
Then began he to upbraid the cities wherein most of his mighty works were done, because they repented not (St. Matt. 11:20, KJV).

Our Simple Lesson
One of the things I learned years ago while being a part of the most wonderful marching band on Earth, the Ocean of Soul, was that everybody who entered the band had to endure the same things. When you were a freshman, you were called a crab. You had to show up for band practice at 5:00 a.m., starting with a two-mile run. You couldn't have a Jeri Curl on your head like I used to have. You had to cut your hair off, wear a white T-shirt and white socks with no stripes. You couldn't walk on the grass. You couldn't have any beverages that had sugar in it, only milk and water. It was like going into the military. And we used to say often, "It's hard but fair. It's sad but true."Today, there are similar sentiments in your passage. It's hard, but it's fair. It's sad, but it's true. The lack of repentance causes you to lose favor in the sight of God. That's hard. God does not hear the hearts of those who are unrepentant when they ask Him to do things like the miraculous. That's hard. Here is what's sad but true: if you do not repent, the repercussions are eternal. It doesn't just stop with those that are miracles. It has eternal consequences. It's hard but fair. It's sad but true.

Our Serious Need To Change
There comes a moment when you realize that change is what you want, not just what you need. You want to change. You're ready for it. Just keep this in mind: your readiness and your willingness hinges on one decision you make for God and then a patience that says, God, when You get ready, I'm willing, and I'm able.

Our Sincere Petition
Thank You, O God, this day for Your love that never ceases, for Your mercies that are made new, and for Your kindness, Lord Jesus, and compassions that never fail. God, I lift those in my life who have not yet repented, and I pray that they find Your grace and love the same way I did.

In The Name of Jesus, Amen.

WEEK 14: They Wouldn't, So He Didn't
Week 14 Conclusion

HIGHER THAN THE TOP
HT3

Life Application

Imagine for a moment that God was wearing handcuffs. Wait, I know this is a far-fetched picture, but just use your sanctified imagination. Imagine, for a moment, God sitting on the throne, wearing handcuffs. His hands want to touch, but they won't. His hands want to heal, but they don't. His hands want to rectify, renew, revive, restore, and redeem things, but they no longer touch because the handcuffs that are on His hands have been placed by you and your spirit of disobedience and non-repentance. God wants to do more for you in your life than you could ever possibly imagine. But there are times when our disbelief, doubt, disobedience, and lack of repentance place handcuffs on His divine actions and activity.

Here is my moment that takes your faith higher than the top today. Use your faith in God. Repent of sins known and unknown. Open your life for the servitude of God in a way that it requires a sacrifice. Serve Him personally so that His hands are loosed and His touch becomes real, so that your life becomes a witness of the grace He personifies, and that the Spirit of the Living God would rest, rule, and remain with you as you seek to serve Him each and every day.

WEEK 15: All You Have to do is R.S.V.P.

Day 1

God's Word For You Today: THE INVITATIONS HAVE GONE OUT

Our Scripture
The Lord is not slack concerning his promise, as some men count slackness; but is longsuffering to us-ward, not willing that any should perish, but that all should come to repentance (2 Pet. 3:9, KJV).

Our Simple Lesson
One day, I had a conversation with an atheist who challenged me regarding the goodness of God. His contention was that either God had all power and was not good or that God was good but simply didn't have all power. This gentleman had concluded the former, that God had all power but was simply not that good. He said to me, in short, "if God was so good, then why all the evil on the Earth? Why all the bad things, the horrible happenings, the global things that are nothing more but complete disasters on the earth?" My answer was simple and yet very, very profound. I simply told this gentleman that God has sent out the invitations for people to join Him, and we keep rejecting Him, and what we see on Earth is the result of people who have told God no instead of simply RSVPing because the invitations have already gone out.

Our Serious Need To Change
In what way have you rejected the goodness of God in your life, where you can simply look at what He desires for you, and you told Him no? God yearns to bless you. According to your scripture study this week in 2 Peter 3:9, the Lord wants none to perish. None! The Lord wants all to come to repentance and find salvation in Him, but some people choose to ignore the invite.

Our Sincere Petition
I thank You, Lord, today for inviting a person like me to be a part of a Kingdom like Yours. I received the invite, and I want You to know You are not just some carpenter from Galilee to me. You are my king, and I am a citizen of your kingdom.

In The Name of Jesus, Amen.

WEEK 15: All You Have to do is R.S.V.P.
Day 2

God's Word For You Today: HE'S A PROMISE KEEPER

Our Scripture
The Lord is not slack concerning his promise, as some men count slackness; but is longsuffering to us-ward, not willing that any should perish, but that all should come to repentance (2 Pet. 3:9, KJV).

Our Simple Lesson
My father, S.V. Adolph Sr, had many admirable traits. Dad worked hard. My father was a family man who sacrificed everything for his wife and his children. I can remember vividly my daddy wearing a black suit until it began shining. It looked like silk, but it was actually polyester, and he had worn it too long. But I can recall during those same seasons, us having wonderful clothes: penny loafers, Levi 501, buttoned-down blue jeans and shirts, and Izod sneakers. It was because he was the kind of dad who would sacrifice for the good of his own. You see, my father was a promise keeper. He was a man who, if he made a promise to you, would do everything in his power to keep it. As Peter writes this magnificent epistle in this second letter that he pens, he makes it clear that the Lord, our Eternal Father, is not slack regarding His promises. If God made you a promise, it's like Oprah Winfrey writing you a check, but on a much larger account because, unlike Oprah, He is from everlasting to everlasting. If God tells you "I will," there is nothing on Earth, in Heaven, or in hell that can reverse it. It shall come to pass. The blessing of your text today is that it is God's desire that none should perish, but He leaves the choice and the recourse to human volition. So all you have to do is make the right choice, and the end benefit is the bounty and blessing of a promise God will not fall short on.

Our Serious Need To Change
There are moments of change in everyone's life, including yours. Take a moment, as we share this time of devotion together, to look at places where it seems that you need to make changes and simply remind yourself that God made you a promise to help you work out your salvation with fear and trembling, and He will do just that.

Our Sincere Petition
Master from on high today, I present to You my human flaws, indignities, and moments of human failure. Take them, I pray. Bathe them in Your forgiveness. Hold fast to Your promise that if I confess them, You will forgive them. In The Name of Jesus, Amen.

WEEK 15: All You Have to do is R.S.V.P.

Day 3

God's Word For You Today: I'M STILL WAITING

Our Scripture
The Lord is not slack concerning his promise, as some men count slackness; but is longsuffering to us-ward, not willing that any should perish, but that all should come to repentance (2 Pet. 3:9, KJV).

Our Simple Lesson
When you hear the words, "I'm still waiting," you often think about things you are waiting on from God that you don't have yet, the miracle that you need, the blessing that you want, the house that you've been trying to get, the things that you've been trying to seize, the doors you've been waiting to open, the ways you've been waiting for Him to make for you. When you hear the words, "I'm still waiting," it seems as if you are waiting on God. But what if you could see it from God's perspective? Could it be that God is waiting on you? The truth of the matter is that God waits for your repentance. He yearns for you to turn to Him and say to Him, God, I need You, and I cannot do this without You. He waits patiently. The text today says He is long-suffering. You can simply put those words in reverse and say God suffers long. It's a way of saying He is so patient that He makes patience have patience. God has more time to wait than you do, so the truth of the matter is He can be patient beyond your wildest imagination. The good news is the wait has not stopped because you are worth waiting for.

Our Serious Need To Change
If God is waiting to bless you, what is He waiting for you to do? What is He waiting for you to change? Today would be a fabulous day for you to make those changes and say, "God, today I say to You, Your wait is over."

Our Sincere Petition
Bless the Lord, O my soul, and all that's within me, bless His holy name. Thank you, O God, for never giving up on me. And thank You, O God, for not stopping the wait but continuing while I need more of Your mercy to make it each day. Hallelujah, Lord Jesus, for the changes I am making and for those that are yet to come. May they bring You glory, and may I become more like Your Son in the process.

In The Name of Jesus, Amen.

WEEK 15: All You Have to do is R.S.V.P.

Day 4

God's Word For You Today: YOUR CHANCE TO CHANGE COULD BE HAPPENING RIGHT NOW

Our Scripture
The Lord is not slack concerning his promise, as some men count slackness; but is longsuffering to us-ward, not willing that any should perish, but that all should come to repentance (2 Pet. 3:9, KJV).

Our Simple Lesson
The message of 2 Peter 3:9 at its core is simply this: your chance to change could be happening right now. The verbs that are used in this passage are in the present tense and the active voice. It suggests that actions are happening now that you could be totally unaware of. God does not want anyone to perish. God wants everyone to come to repentance. God is long-suffering and does not slack regarding his promises. It's another way of simply saying he's waiting. He's patient. His love is real. His grace is amazing. His mercies are made new each morning, and His hands are not slack concerning the promises He's made towards you. If He has promised forgiveness, then you are already forgiven. If He has promised love, it goes beyond human understanding and decree. And if He has promised grace, you will discover it is still amazing. The chance to change is happening, and it is happening now. You just must make up your mind. You're willing to receive it, and you accept it by simply repenting.

Our Serious Need To Change
Not long ago, I was reading a book by Watchman Nee entitled "The Normal Christian Life," in which a strong and a weak swimmer dove into a ravine to reach the other side. The strong swimmer made it across, and the weak swimmer began floundering in the middle of the ravine. The strong swimmer watched the weak swimmer go up and down and then, ultimately, under the current, which he dove in to save him. He brought him back to the seashore, and then others asked him, "Why did you wait so long to help him?" The strong swimmer simply replied, "I had to wait until he was weak enough to accept the changes I would make in his life." Here is a question that I want to ask you: Are you weak enough for God to save you from the current of sin that sometimes overwhelms you? Are you weak enough yet for God to save and deliver? When you become weak enough for God to bless, you will discover grace's strength for your life.

WEEK 15: All You Have to do is R.S.V.P.

Our Sincere Petition

Master, I plan to serve You until I can serve no longer. I realize, Lord, that in times when I thought I was really strong, I was actually weak. Today, O God, I'm weak enough for You to bless, able enough to use, weak enough to save, and willing enough to work for You. Thank You for keeping me is my plea and my prayer.

In The Name of Jesus, Amen.

WEEK 15: All You Have to do is R.S.V.P.

Day 5

God's Word For You Today: WHEN YOU TRANSLATE THE WORD "ALL" IT MEANS "ALL"

Our Scripture
The Lord is not slack concerning his promise, as some men count slackness; but is longsuffering to us-ward, not willing that any should perish, but that all should come to repentance (2 Pet. 3:9, KJV).

Our Simple Lesson
Whenever you translate the word "all" mentioned in this passage, it says, "...*but that all should come to repentance*". When you translate the word "all," it means "all" in Greek, Hebrew, and Latin. The desire, then, of God is for all to be saved, for all to be in Heaven, for all to be redeemed, for all to be renewed. After all, there is nothing before all, there is nothing after all, there is nothing above all, there is nothing beneath all because all means all.

It stands to reason that you would grapple with the question, why will there be people in hell, and why are there people who reject God, and why are there those who refuse His grace and don't come to know His mercy? It's because some people refuse to repent. There will always be those who say, "I'm not going to do it. I refuse to do it. And no matter how much you want to tell me how great this God of yours is, I will never serve Him".

Our Serious Need To Change
Right now, you should be really grateful you're not one of the people who refuses the love of God but receive it every day. In fact, you being able to take a moment and have devotion to God today, as you study this lesson, is proof that you are a benefactor of the grace, mercy, and love of God.

Our Sincere Petition
Let my light so shine, O God, amongst men that they might see You and not me. Have my friends, my neighbors, my coworkers, and Lord, even my foes who appear to be friends, come to know You because of what I have in You and for what You are doing in me. And, God, on the day they do come, I will rejoice because it's You that they've been seeking the entire time.

In The Name of Jesus, Amen.

WEEK 15: All You Have to do is R.S.V.P.

Day 6

God's Word For You Today: SOME PEOPLE JUST WON'T ACT RIGHT

Our Scripture
The Lord is not slack concerning his promise, as some men count slackness; but is longsuffering to us-ward, not willing that any should perish, but that all should come to repentance (2 Pet. 3:9, KJV).

Our Simple Lesson
Some people on Earth will never do right. If they see a sign that reads 55 miles per hour, they're going to go 70. If a doctor tells them not to eat red meat, they go and order a porterhouse steak. If there are people who tell them, "You can't have this because it's bad for you," they go and order three of them and then decide to chew and swallow. Some people just won't act right. The truth of the matter is, even for those who don't do right, there is a way to get right. Repentance is the way you do that. "*The Lord is not slack concerning his promise,*" says Peter, "*as some men count slackness.*" What he's saying is God's promises are not like those of men. Men change their minds, but God's mind is made up for you. And what God does for you triggers and places itself on the turntable of sincere, devout repentance. Feel sorry about your past. Feel sad about your current sins, but then change your mind about them, and your mind will change your actions. Your action will change your attitude. Your attitude will change your altitude. Your altitude will change your outcome. And your outcome will help you overcome because God is on your side. It's profound and prolific. It's simple, but it works. Repentance is how people who won't act right get right, and there is no other way.

Our Serious Need To Change
When you look at your life as a person, it is easy to admit that none of us are perfect, but it is difficult to confront some things that are hard for you to change. In many instances, the difficulty to deal with these changes effectively comes from the fact that there are some struggles you like to have. Some bad habits you want to hold on to. Today, you should make a decision to let go of anything that won't truthfully benefit you in the eyes of God. To do so is not for God's good; it's for yours.

WEEK 15: All You Have to do is R.S.V.P.

Our Sincere Petition

I will bless the Lord at all times. His praise shall continually be in my mouth. That is my prayer today. That is my praise today. As I seek, oh God, to not just want to do right but to be right, give me the strength to be right so that I act right.

In The Name of Jesus, Amen.

WEEK 15: All You Have to do is R.S.V.P.

Day 7

God's Word For You Today: DELIVERANCE WORKS BEST WHEN YOU COOPERATE

Our Scripture
The Lord is not slack concerning his promise, as some men count slackness; but is longsuffering to us-ward, not willing that any should perish, but that all should come to repentance (2 Pet. 3:9, KJV).

Our Simple Lesson
As you have studied 2 Peter 3:9, you must conclude the following: that God is a gracious, strong, and mighty deliverer whose truthfulness and veracity makes Him one who is a promise keeper, not a promise breaker, one who is willing to be patient with you, even when what you are doing is not pleasing to Him. Instead of expressing wrath and judgment and anger, He gives you mercies that are still new each morning, a willingness that's within His heart that none should perish but that all should come to a place of repentance where they've changed their minds about Him. What a loving God! But here is the internal part of the passage that should make all of us rejoice: God delivers, and He does so well, but deliverance works best when you cooperate. It is one thing for somebody to try to save you from a burning building. It's another thing for you to run back into the flames, not wanting to come out. It is one thing for someone to enjoy a better life for you; it is another thing for you to return to the slop of your life and say, I was more comfortable here. God delivered His people from Egypt, but there is still some Egypt in the people who want to go back to a former lifestyle. Hear these words of wisdom today: God delivers much easier for those who cooperate, and when you are offered, don't go back.

Our Serious Need To Change
The enemy would love for you to go back to your former lifestyle. He would celebrate. He would just cheer you on. It would make you uncomfortable to know that the thing that God delivered you from still awaits your new arrival. But here's what you should do today. Make up your mind that reverse is a curse, and move forward.

Our Sincere Petition
Thank You, Lord Jesus, for allowing me time to repent. Thank You for the prayers of repentance You have heard me pray. I celebrate the changes in my life that You are making because, without You, I cannot, but with You, I can. In The Name of Jesus, Amen.

WEEK 15: All You Have to do is R.S.V.P.

Week 15 Conclusion

HIGHER THAN THE TOP
HT3

Life Application

You have taken a 15-week journey through a categorical study of repentance. You've looked at word studies in Greek, Hebrew, and Latin. You have taken the time to study passages every single day for 15 weeks. Here is what makes your faith in God right now higher than the top: You have become sensitive to your sins and struggles. Be slow to point a finger at the flaws of other Christians. After all, we're not at the same level of maturity. Be cautious about the demonic activity that causes disobedience in others. Be careful and soft when it regards human flaws, but be firm in the faith as it relates to standing for the Lord and getting others to stand with you.

Most importantly, as a member of God's Church on Earth, serve God with a fervor and a faithfulness that says I'm indebted to Him, that even though I've changed my mind about my previous king and my previous kingdom, I have a new excitement about my new King and my new Kingdom. After all, my new King has a name that is above every name, that at the mentioning of His name, one of these days, every knee shall bow, and every tongue shall confess that He is Lord, the glory of God the Father. I serve that King because He has died for me. I owe this King because He has done so much for me. And with my life, I will worship my King until the day I can meet Him face to face, fall at His feet, and hear His voice declare over my life, "Servant, well done."

I am more conscious and cautious now than I have ever been that sin must be repented of, that I must change from those things that are not pleasing to God. With the strength He gives me, I will make every change. With the wisdom that He blesses me with, I will do my best. And in those areas where I am too weak to handle it, I will depend on His strength to bring me out.

These are the words of repentance that have been printed for you. Thank you for taking the time to go through this 15-week study. May the words and the wisdom that has been expressed in this literary work cause you to walk closer with the LORD than you have ever walked before in your life.

My concluding word today is this: that every hand that touches this book, every eye that reads it will one day reach the celestial shores of New Jerusalem, where we can see each other, where

WEEK 15: All You Have to do is R.S.V.P.

sin will no longer abound, where wickedness will cease from troubling, and weariness shall never bother us again, where every person who reads this book would make it to Heaven because they have lived the life of repentance that pleases God.

In The Name of Jesus, Amen.

Antioch Missionary Baptist Church
3920 W. Cardinal Drive Beaumont, TX 77705
Dr. John R. Adolph, Pastor
Website www.antiochbmt.org
FaceBook: Antioch Missionary Baptist Church
IG: @antiochbmt

Worship Service
Every Sunday at 8:00 am & 10:00 am
Virtual and Personal
Website: www.antiochbmt.org
YouTube: John R. Adolph Ministries LLC.

War Room Prayer Call
Every Wednesday at 7:00 am
YouTube: John R. Adolph Ministries LLC.

Bible Study
Every Thursday at 6:00 pm
Virtual and Personal
Website: www.antiochbmt.org
YouTube: John R. Adolph Ministries LLC.

John R. Adolph Ministries LLC.
The Message. The Ministry. The Man.
Website: www.jradolph.com

YouTube: John R. Adolph Ministries LLC.

FaceBook: John R. Adolph Ministries LLC.

IG: @iamjradolph

Other Books and Articles by John R. Adolph

I'm Changing the Game
Not Without A Fight
I'm Coming Out of This
Just Stick to the Script
Victorious Christian Living Volume I
Victorious Christian Living Volume II
Let Me Encourage You Volume I
Let Me Encourage You Volume II
The Him Book I
The Him Book II | The Anthology
Get Ready For Battle
Marriage Is For Losers
Celibacy Is For Fools
I Want Some Too
Victory: Ten Fundamental Beliefs That Eradicate Defeat in the Life of a Christian
Better Together
Based On A True Story
Back To The Table
Help Me Handle This

Articles-Zondervan Press
He Loves Me, He Loves Me, He Loves Me
I'm Certain That He Loves Me
His Love Made The Difference
God's Mind Is Made Up, He Loves You

To purchase additional copies of this book or other books by Dr Adolph or visit Amazon.com our bookstore website at:
www.advbookstore.com

*A*dvantage BOOKS

Orlando, Florida, USA
"we bring dreams to life"™
www.advbookstore.com

www.ingramcontent.com/pod-product-compliance
Lightning Source LLC
Chambersburg PA
CBHW081234170426
43198CB00017B/2760